The Language of Architecture

Decoding the Elements of Design

Dean Pearce

The presentation of the information is without contract or any type of guarantee assurance. The trademarks that are used are without any consent, and the publication of the trademark is without permission or backing by the trademark owner. All trademarks and brands within this book are for clarifying purposes only and are the owned by the owners themselves, not affiliated with this document.

Table of Contents

Chapter 1

Introduction to Architectural Language

Understanding Architectural Terminology

Architectural terminology serves as the foundation for understanding the intricate world of design and construction. It is a language that architects, designers, and builders use to communicate ideas, concepts, and technical details. Mastering this language is essential for anyone involved in the field, as it allows for precise communication and a shared understanding of the elements that make up the built environment.

At the heart of architectural terminology are the basic elements that define a structure. These include terms like "façade," which refers to the exterior face of a building, often the most visually prominent aspect. The façade can be adorned with various materials and styles, reflecting the building's aesthetic and functional intentions. Another fundamental term is "plan," which denotes a horizontal section of a building, typically viewed from above. Plans are crucial for visualizing the layout and spatial organization of a structure.

Moving beyond the basics, architectural terminology delves into more complex concepts such as "axial symmetry," a design principle where elements are arranged around a central axis, creating balance and harmony. This principle is often employed in classical architecture, where symmetry and proportion are paramount. Similarly, "asymmetry" is used to describe a lack of symmetry, often resulting in dynamic and visually interesting compositions.

The language of architecture also encompasses the various styles and movements that have shaped the built environment over time. Terms like "Gothic," "Baroque," and "Modernism" evoke distinct architectural styles, each with its own set of characteristics and historical context. Understanding these styles is crucial for appreciating the evolution of architecture and the cultural influences that have shaped it.

In addition to styles, architectural terminology includes the various components that make up a building. For instance, "cornice" refers to the decorative molding that crowns a building, while "pediment" describes the triangular gable found above the entrance of classical structures. These elements not only serve functional purposes but also contribute to the overall aesthetic of a building.

The terminology also extends to the materials used in construction. Words like "masonry," "concrete," and "steel" describe the building blocks of architecture, each with its own properties and applications. Understanding these materials is essential for making informed decisions about the structural integrity and sustainability of a design.

Architectural terminology is not limited to the physical aspects of a building; it also encompasses the spatial and experiential qualities of architecture.

Terms like "circulation" refer to the movement of people through a space, while "threshold" describes the transition between different areas. These concepts are vital for designing spaces that are both functional and engaging.

The language of architecture is constantly evolving, reflecting changes in technology, culture, and society. New terms emerge as architects push the boundaries of design and explore innovative approaches to building. For example, "parametric design" is a relatively recent term that describes a process where algorithms are used to generate complex forms and structures. This approach has opened up new possibilities for architects, allowing for greater flexibility and creativity in design.

Understanding architectural terminology is not just about memorizing a list of words; it is about grasping the concepts and ideas that underpin the built environment. It requires an appreciation for the history and evolution of architecture, as well as an awareness of the cultural and technological forces that continue to shape it.

For those new to the field, mastering architectural terminology can be a daunting task. However, it is an essential step in becoming proficient in the language of design. By familiarizing oneself with the key terms and concepts, one can begin to engage with architecture on a deeper level, appreciating the nuances and complexities that define this dynamic field.

In practice, architectural terminology serves as a bridge between the abstract world of design and the tangible reality of construction. It allows architects to convey their vision to clients, builders, and other stakeholders, ensuring that everyone involved in a project is on the same page. This shared language is crucial for the successful execution of a design, as it facilitates clear communication and collaboration.

Moreover, understanding architectural terminology can enhance one's ability to critique and analyze buildings. By recognizing the elements and principles that define a structure, one can assess its effectiveness in terms of aesthetics, functionality, and sustainability. This critical perspective is valuable for both professionals and enthusiasts, as it fosters a deeper appreciation for the art and science of architecture.

The Evolution of Architectural Language

Architecture, as a discipline, has always been a reflection of the society and culture from which it emerges. The language of architecture, therefore, is not static; it evolves alongside the civilizations that create it. This evolution is marked by shifts in design principles, technological advancements, and cultural influences, each contributing to the rich tapestry of architectural expression.

In ancient times, architecture was primarily a means of survival and utility. Structures were built to provide shelter and protection, with little emphasis on aesthetics. However, as societies grew more complex, so did their architectural expressions. The ancient

Egyptians, for instance, developed a highly symbolic architectural language, with monumental structures like the pyramids serving as both tombs and symbols of divine power. Their use of massive stone blocks and precise geometric forms demonstrated an understanding of both engineering and the spiritual significance of architecture.

The Greeks further advanced architectural language by introducing the concept of order and proportion. Their development of the classical orders—Doric, Ionic, and Corinthian—provided a framework for architectural design that emphasized harmony and balance. These principles were not merely aesthetic; they were deeply rooted in the Greek philosophy of beauty and the pursuit of perfection. The Parthenon, with its precise proportions and intricate detailing, stands as a testament to the Greek mastery of architectural language.

As the Roman Empire rose to prominence, it absorbed and adapted the architectural language of the Greeks, infusing it with their own innovations. The Romans were pioneers in the use of concrete, which allowed them to create vast and complex structures such as the Colosseum and the Pantheon. Their architectural language was characterized by grandeur and functionality, with an emphasis on engineering prowess and the ability to manipulate space on an unprecedented scale.

The fall of the Roman Empire marked a shift in architectural language as Europe entered the Middle Ages. During this period, architecture became heavily influenced by religious and feudal systems. The Gothic style emerged, characterized by pointed arches, ribbed vaults, and flying buttresses. This architectural language was not only a reflection of the religious fervor of the time but also a response to the technical challenges of building taller and more light-filled structures. The cathedrals of this era, such as Notre-Dame de Paris, are masterpieces of Gothic architecture, embodying both spiritual aspiration and structural innovation.

The Renaissance brought about a revival of classical architectural language, as architects sought to rediscover the principles of ancient Greece and Rome. This period was marked by a renewed focus on symmetry, proportion, and geometry, as well as the use of perspective in architectural design. Architects like Filippo Brunelleschi and Andrea Palladio were instrumental in shaping the Renaissance architectural language, which emphasized clarity, order, and the harmonious integration of form and function.

The Baroque period followed, characterized by dramatic expressions and elaborate ornamentation. This architectural language was a response to the rigid formalism of the Renaissance, embracing movement, contrast, and theatricality. Baroque architecture, as seen in structures like St. Peter's Basilica in Rome, sought to evoke emotion and awe, using dynamic forms and opulent details to create a sense of grandeur and splendor.

The Industrial Revolution of the 19th century brought about another significant evolution in architectural language. The advent of new materials and technologies, such as iron and steel, allowed architects to explore new forms and structures. The language of architecture during this period was marked by a tension between tradition and innovation, as architects grappled with the possibilities and challenges of industrialization. The Crystal Palace, designed by Joseph Paxton for the Great Exhibition of 1851, exemplifies this era's architectural language, with its use of prefabricated iron and glass to create a vast, light-filled space.

The 20th century saw the emergence of modernism, a radical departure from historical styles and ornamentation. Modernist architects, such as Le Corbusier and Ludwig Mies van der Rohe, sought to create a new architectural language that embraced simplicity, functionality, and the honest expression of materials. This language was characterized by clean lines, open spaces, and a focus on the needs of the modern individual. The Villa Savoye and the Barcelona Pavilion are iconic examples of modernist architecture, embodying the principles of form following function and the integration of indoor and outdoor spaces.

As the century progressed, postmodernism emerged as a reaction against the perceived austerity of modernism. This architectural language embraced eclecticism, irony, and a return to ornamentation, often incorporating historical references and playful elements. Architects like Robert Venturi and Michael Graves challenged the conventions of modernism, creating buildings that were both functional and expressive.

Today, the language of architecture continues to evolve, influenced by globalization, sustainability, and technological advancements. Contemporary architects are exploring new materials, digital design tools, and

innovative construction techniques to create buildings
that respond to the challenges of the 21st century. The
language of architecture is increasingly focused on
sustainability, with an emphasis on energy efficiency,
environmental impact, and the use of renewable
resources. This shift is reflected in the design of
buildings like the Bosco Verticale in Milan, which
integrates greenery into its structure to promote
biodiversity and improve air quality.

The Role of Language in Design Communication

Language serves as a vital conduit in the realm of
design communication, bridging the gap between
abstract concepts and tangible creations. It is through
language that designers articulate their visions,
convey their intentions, and collaborate with clients,
colleagues, and stakeholders. The role of language in
design communication is multifaceted, encompassing
verbal, written, and visual forms, each contributing to
the clarity and effectiveness of the design process.

At the heart of design communication lies the ability
to translate complex ideas into accessible language.
Designers often grapple with abstract concepts, such
as aesthetics, functionality, and user experience. To
communicate these ideas effectively, they must
employ language that resonates with diverse
audiences, from technical experts to laypersons. This
requires a keen understanding of the audience's needs
and perspectives, as well as the ability to adapt
language to suit different contexts.

Verbal communication plays a crucial role in the design process, particularly during collaborative discussions and presentations. Designers must articulate their ideas clearly and persuasively, using language to build consensus and foster understanding. This involves not only the choice of words but also the tone, pace, and delivery of speech. Effective verbal communication can inspire confidence, encourage feedback, and facilitate problem-solving, ultimately leading to more successful design outcomes.

Written communication is equally important in design, serving as a record of ideas, decisions, and specifications. Designers use written language to create design briefs, proposals, reports, and documentation, each requiring a different level of detail and formality. A well-crafted design brief, for example, provides a clear and concise overview of the project's objectives, constraints, and deliverables, guiding the design process and ensuring alignment among all parties involved. Precision and clarity in written communication are essential, as they help prevent misunderstandings and ensure that all stakeholders have a shared understanding of the project's goals.

Visual language is another critical component of design communication, encompassing sketches, diagrams, models, and digital renderings. Visuals serve as a universal language, transcending linguistic barriers and allowing designers to convey complex ideas quickly and effectively. They provide a tangible representation of abstract concepts, enabling stakeholders to visualize the design and provide feedback. The use of visual language is particularly important in design fields such as architecture, industrial design, and graphic design, where spatial relationships and aesthetics play a central role.

The integration of verbal, written, and visual language is essential for effective design communication. Designers must be adept at weaving these forms of language together, creating a cohesive narrative that guides the design process from concept to completion. This requires not only technical skills but also creativity and empathy, as designers must anticipate the needs and expectations of their audience and tailor their communication accordingly.

In addition to these traditional forms of language, digital communication tools have become increasingly important in the design process. Platforms such as video conferencing, collaborative software, and social media enable designers to communicate and collaborate with global teams in real-time. These tools offer new opportunities for interaction and feedback, allowing designers to share ideas, gather input, and iterate on designs more efficiently. However, they also present challenges, as designers must navigate the nuances of digital communication and ensure that their message is conveyed accurately and effectively.

The role of language in design communication extends beyond the immediate design team, encompassing interactions with clients, users, and the broader community. Designers must be able to communicate the value and impact of their work, advocating for design solutions that meet the needs of users and contribute to the greater good. This requires a deep understanding of the social, cultural, and environmental context in which the design operates, as well as the ability to articulate the design's benefits and implications in a compelling and relatable manner.

Empathy is a key component of effective design communication, as it enables designers to connect with their audience on a deeper level. By understanding the emotions, motivations, and concerns of their audience, designers can craft language that resonates and inspires action. This empathetic approach is particularly important in user-centered design, where the success of a design hinges on its ability to meet the needs and expectations of its users.

The iterative nature of the design process also underscores the importance of language in design communication. As designs evolve and change, so too must the language used to describe them. Designers must be flexible and adaptable, continuously refining their communication to reflect new insights, feedback, and developments. This iterative approach ensures that all stakeholders remain informed and engaged throughout the design process, fostering collaboration and innovation.

Bridging the Gap Architects and Clients

The relationship between architects and clients is a delicate dance, a partnership that requires mutual understanding, trust, and effective communication. Bridging the gap between these two parties is essential for the successful realization of any architectural project. This chapter delves into the nuances of this relationship, offering insights and strategies to foster collaboration and ensure that both architects and clients are aligned in their vision and goals.

At the core of the architect-client relationship is the need for clear and open communication. Architects must be adept at listening to their clients, understanding their needs, desires, and constraints. This involves more than just hearing words; it requires an empathetic approach to grasp the underlying motivations and aspirations that drive the client's vision. By establishing a strong foundation of communication from the outset, architects can ensure that they are on the same page as their clients, minimizing misunderstandings and potential conflicts down the line.

One of the key challenges in bridging the gap between architects and clients is managing expectations. Clients often come to the table with preconceived notions of what their project should look like, influenced by personal tastes, trends, or previous experiences. Architects, on the other hand, bring their expertise, creativity, and understanding of technical and regulatory constraints. Balancing these perspectives requires a delicate negotiation, where architects must educate clients about the realities of the design and construction process while remaining open to their input and ideas.

To effectively manage expectations, architects should engage clients in a collaborative design process. This involves involving clients in key decision-making stages, presenting them with options, and explaining the implications of each choice. By demystifying the design process and making clients active participants, architects can build trust and foster a sense of ownership in the project. This collaborative approach not only enhances the final design but also strengthens the relationship between architects and clients, as both parties feel valued and heard.

Another important aspect of bridging the gap is addressing the financial aspects of a project. Budget constraints are a common source of tension between architects and clients, as clients may have ambitious visions that exceed their financial means. Architects must be transparent about costs from the outset, providing clients with realistic estimates and helping them prioritize their needs and wants. By working together to develop a feasible budget, architects and clients can avoid financial surprises and ensure that the project remains on track.

In addition to communication and financial considerations, architects must also navigate the emotional landscape of their clients. Architectural projects are often deeply personal, as they involve creating spaces where clients will live, work, or engage with their communities. As such, clients may have strong emotional attachments to certain ideas or elements of the design. Architects must be sensitive to these emotions, acknowledging their importance while guiding clients towards practical and sustainable solutions. This requires a balance of empathy and professionalism, as architects must respect their clients' feelings while maintaining the integrity of the design.

Cultural differences can also play a role in the architect-client relationship, particularly in projects involving international clients or diverse communities. Architects must be culturally aware and adaptable, recognizing that different cultures may have varying expectations, communication styles, and design preferences. By embracing cultural diversity and incorporating it into the design process, architects can create spaces that are not only functional and aesthetically pleasing but also culturally resonant and inclusive.

Technology can be a valuable tool in bridging the gap between architects and clients. Digital design tools, virtual reality, and 3D modeling allow architects to present their ideas in a more tangible and interactive way, helping clients visualize the final outcome and provide informed feedback. These tools can enhance communication and collaboration, making the design process more transparent and accessible to clients. However, architects must also be mindful of the limitations of technology and ensure that it complements, rather than replaces, personal interactions and discussions.

Ultimately, the success of the architect-client relationship hinges on mutual respect and trust. Architects must respect their clients' vision and values, while clients must trust their architects' expertise and judgment. This requires a commitment to open dialogue, active listening, and a willingness to compromise and adapt. By fostering a collaborative and respectful partnership, architects and clients can bridge the gap between their perspectives and work

together to create spaces that are both beautiful and
functional.

The Influence of Culture on Architectural Language

Architecture, as a form of expression, is deeply
intertwined with the cultural fabric of the societies it
serves. The influence of culture on architectural
language is profound, shaping not only the aesthetic
and functional aspects of buildings but also their
symbolic meanings and social significance. This
chapter delves into the intricate relationship between
culture and architecture, exploring how cultural
values, traditions, and histories manifest in the built
environment.

Cultural identity is often reflected in architectural
styles, materials, and construction techniques. For
instance, the use of local materials and traditional
building methods can convey a sense of place and
continuity with the past. In regions where timber is
abundant, such as Scandinavia, wooden structures are
prevalent, showcasing the resourcefulness and
adaptability of local communities. Similarly, adobe
and mudbrick constructions in arid regions like North
Africa and the Middle East highlight the ingenuity of
using available resources to create sustainable and
climate-responsive architecture.

The symbolism embedded in architectural forms is
another testament to the influence of culture.
Religious and spiritual beliefs often dictate the design
of sacred spaces, with architectural elements serving

as metaphors for divine principles. The soaring spires of Gothic cathedrals, for example, are not merely structural features but are intended to draw the eye heavenward, symbolizing the aspiration towards the divine. In contrast, the horizontal lines and open spaces of Shinto shrines in Japan reflect a harmonious relationship with nature, emphasizing simplicity and tranquility.

Cultural narratives and historical events also leave their mark on architectural language. Monuments and memorials serve as physical embodiments of collective memory, commemorating significant events or figures. The Vietnam Veterans Memorial in Washington, D.C., with its stark black granite walls inscribed with the names of fallen soldiers, is a poignant example of how architecture can evoke powerful emotions and foster reflection. Similarly, the intricate carvings and bas-reliefs of Angkor Wat in Cambodia narrate stories from Hindu mythology, preserving cultural heritage through architectural artistry.

Urban planning and the organization of space within cities are influenced by cultural norms and social structures. In many traditional societies, the layout of settlements reflects hierarchical relationships and communal values. The concentric design of the Forbidden City in Beijing, with its central axis and symmetrical arrangement, embodies the Confucian ideals of order and harmony. Conversely, the organic and labyrinthine streets of medieval European towns reveal a more spontaneous and adaptive approach to urban development, shaped by the needs and interactions of their inhabitants.

The globalization of architecture has led to a dynamic exchange of ideas and styles, resulting in a rich tapestry of cultural influences. However, this phenomenon also raises questions about the preservation of cultural identity in the face of homogenization. The proliferation of glass-and-steel skyscrapers in cities worldwide, while emblematic of modernity and progress, often leads to a loss of local character and distinctiveness. Architects and planners must navigate this tension, finding ways to integrate global trends with local traditions to create spaces that resonate with their cultural context.

Cultural diversity can be a source of inspiration and innovation in architecture. By embracing multicultural influences, architects can create designs that celebrate the richness of human experience. The Sydney Opera House, with its iconic sail-like shells, draws inspiration from both Western and Eastern architectural traditions, resulting in a structure that is both universally recognizable and uniquely Australian. Such hybrid designs demonstrate the potential for architecture to transcend cultural boundaries and foster cross-cultural understanding.

The role of architecture in shaping cultural identity extends beyond aesthetics and symbolism. Buildings and spaces influence how people interact, perceive themselves, and relate to their environment. The design of public spaces, for example, can promote social cohesion and inclusivity by providing venues for community gatherings and cultural events. Conversely, poorly designed or inaccessible spaces can exacerbate social divisions and marginalize certain groups. Architects have a responsibility to consider the social and cultural implications of their work, ensuring that their designs contribute positively to the communities they serve.

Education and awareness are crucial in fostering an appreciation for the cultural dimensions of architecture. By studying the architectural heritage of different cultures, architects can gain insights into the values and aspirations that shape the built environment. This knowledge can inform contemporary design practices, encouraging architects to create spaces that are not only functional and aesthetically pleasing but also culturally meaningful and contextually appropriate.

Chapter 2

The Foundations of Design

Principles of Design Balance and Proportion

Design balance and proportion are fundamental principles that underpin the creation of harmonious and aesthetically pleasing compositions. These principles are not confined to any single discipline but are universally applicable across various fields, including architecture, graphic design, fashion, and interior design. Understanding and applying these principles can transform a chaotic arrangement into a cohesive and visually engaging masterpiece.

Balance in design refers to the distribution of visual weight within a composition. It is the equilibrium achieved when elements are arranged in a way that feels stable and pleasing to the eye. There are several types of balance that designers can employ, each with its own unique characteristics and effects.

Symmetrical balance, also known as formal balance, is achieved when elements are mirrored on either side of a central axis. This type of balance is often associated with order, stability, and formality. It is commonly used in classical architecture, where buildings are designed with a central entrance flanked by identical wings. The Parthenon in Athens is a quintessential example of symmetrical balance, with its evenly spaced columns and harmonious proportions creating a sense of grandeur and permanence.

Asymmetrical balance, or informal balance, involves the arrangement of dissimilar elements to create a sense of equilibrium. This type of balance is more dynamic and visually interesting, as it relies on the careful placement of elements with varying sizes, shapes, and colors to achieve harmony. Asymmetrical balance is often used in modern art and design, where the juxtaposition of contrasting elements can evoke a sense of movement and energy. The works of abstract expressionist painters, such as Jackson Pollock, exemplify the use of asymmetrical balance to create compositions that are both balanced and vibrant.

Radial balance is achieved when elements radiate outward from a central point, creating a circular composition. This type of balance is often found in nature, as seen in the petals of a flower or the spokes of a wheel. Radial balance can be used to draw attention to a focal point, creating a sense of unity and cohesion. In design, radial balance is often employed in logos and mandalas, where the repetition of elements around a central point creates a harmonious and captivating pattern.

Proportion, on the other hand, refers to the relationship between the sizes of different elements within a composition. It is the principle that ensures that all parts of a design relate to each other in a way that feels natural and balanced. Proportion is closely linked to the concept of scale, which refers to the size of an object in relation to its surroundings.

The golden ratio, a mathematical ratio of approximately 1:1.618, is a classic example of proportion in design. This ratio has been used for centuries to create compositions that are aesthetically pleasing and harmonious. The golden ratio can be found in the proportions of the human body, the spirals of seashells, and the architecture of iconic structures such as the Great Pyramid of Giza. By applying the golden ratio to design, artists and architects can create compositions that resonate with a sense of natural beauty and balance.

In addition to the golden ratio, designers often use grids and modular systems to establish proportion within a composition. Grids provide a framework for organizing elements, ensuring that they are aligned and proportionate. This approach is particularly useful in graphic design and typography, where the consistent use of grids can create a sense of order and coherence. The Swiss Style of graphic design, characterized by its use of grids and clean lines, exemplifies the effective use of proportion to create visually appealing layouts.

The interplay between balance and proportion is crucial in achieving a successful design. While balance ensures that elements are distributed evenly, proportion ensures that they relate to each other in a harmonious way. Together, these principles create compositions that are both stable and dynamic, capturing the viewer's attention and guiding their gaze through the design.

Practical application of these principles requires a keen eye and an understanding of the elements at play. Designers must consider factors such as color, texture, and form when arranging elements within a composition. By experimenting with different arrangements and observing the effects of balance and proportion, designers can develop an intuitive sense of what works and what doesn't.

Incorporating balance and proportion into design is not merely a technical exercise but an art form that requires creativity and sensitivity. It is about finding the right combination of elements that resonate with the viewer and evoke the desired emotional response. Whether designing a building, a piece of furniture, or a digital interface, the principles of balance and proportion are essential tools that can elevate a design from ordinary to extraordinary.

The Role of Geometry in Architecture

Geometry has long been a cornerstone of architectural design, serving as both a practical tool and a source of inspiration. From the ancient pyramids of Egypt to the modern skyscrapers that define city skylines, geometry provides the framework upon which architects build their visions. Its role in architecture is multifaceted, encompassing everything from structural integrity to aesthetic appeal.

At its core, geometry is about the relationships between shapes and spaces. In architecture, these relationships are crucial for creating structures that are both functional and beautiful. The use of geometric principles allows architects to design buildings that are not only visually striking but also structurally sound. By understanding the properties of different shapes and how they interact, architects can create designs that maximize space, enhance stability, and optimize the flow of movement within a building.

One of the most iconic examples of geometry in architecture is the use of the triangle. Known for its inherent stability, the triangle is a fundamental shape in structural design. Its ability to distribute weight evenly makes it an ideal choice for creating strong and durable structures. This principle is evident in the design of trusses, which are used to support roofs and bridges. By arranging triangles in a specific pattern, architects can create a framework that is both lightweight and capable of bearing significant loads.

The circle is another geometric shape that has played a significant role in architectural design. Its perfect symmetry and infinite nature have made it a symbol of unity and eternity in various cultures. In architecture, circles are often used to create domes, which are not only visually impressive but also structurally efficient. The Pantheon in Rome, with its massive concrete dome, is a testament to the enduring appeal and practicality of circular geometry. The dome's design allows for an open, unobstructed interior space, while its shape evenly distributes weight, reducing the need for additional support.

Rectangles and squares are perhaps the most common geometric shapes used in architecture. Their simplicity and versatility make them ideal for creating functional spaces. The grid-like layout of many modern cities is a reflection of the practicality of rectangular geometry. By organizing buildings and streets into a series of squares and rectangles, urban planners can create efficient and easily navigable environments. This approach is evident in the design of cities like New York, where the grid system allows for straightforward movement and organization.

Beyond these basic shapes, more complex geometric forms have also found their place in architecture. The use of fractals, for example, has gained popularity in recent years. Fractals are intricate patterns that repeat at different scales, creating a sense of complexity and harmony. Architects have begun to incorporate fractal geometry into their designs to create buildings that are both visually captivating and environmentally responsive. The Eden Project in Cornwall, England, is an example of this approach, with its geodesic domes inspired by the natural fractal patterns found in nature.

The role of geometry in architecture extends beyond the physical structure of buildings. It also influences the way spaces are perceived and experienced. The use of geometric patterns and proportions can evoke specific emotions and create a sense of order and balance. The golden ratio, a mathematical ratio often found in nature, has been used by architects for centuries to create harmonious and aesthetically pleasing designs. This ratio can be seen in the proportions of famous structures such as the Parthenon and the Notre-Dame Cathedral, where it contributes to the overall sense of beauty and symmetry.

In addition to its aesthetic and structural applications, geometry also plays a crucial role in the planning and organization of architectural projects. By using geometric principles, architects can create detailed blueprints and models that guide the construction process. These plans ensure that every element of a building is precisely measured and aligned, reducing the risk of errors and ensuring that the final structure meets the intended design.

The integration of geometry into architecture is not limited to traditional methods. Advances in technology have opened up new possibilities for incorporating complex geometric forms into architectural design. Computer-aided design (CAD) software allows architects to experiment with intricate shapes and patterns that would have been difficult to achieve using traditional techniques. This technology enables architects to push the boundaries of what is possible, creating innovative and futuristic designs that challenge conventional notions of architecture.

Despite the advancements in technology, the fundamental principles of geometry remain as relevant as ever. They provide a foundation upon which architects can build, allowing them to create structures that are both functional and inspiring. By understanding and applying these principles, architects can design buildings that not only meet the practical needs of their occupants but also enrich their lives through beauty and harmony.

Scale and Proportion Creating Harmony

Scale and proportion are fundamental concepts in architecture, serving as the invisible threads that weave together the fabric of a harmonious design. These principles guide architects in creating spaces that resonate with human perception, ensuring that buildings are not only functional but also aesthetically pleasing. By understanding and applying the concepts of scale and proportion, architects can craft environments that evoke a sense of balance and unity.

Scale refers to the size of an object in relation to its surroundings or to the human body. It is a crucial consideration in architectural design, as it influences how a building is perceived and experienced. A structure that is too large or too small in relation to its context can feel overwhelming or insignificant. Therefore, architects must carefully consider the scale of their designs to ensure that they fit harmoniously within their environment.

One of the most famous examples of scale in architecture is the use of human scale. This approach involves designing buildings and spaces that are proportionate to the human body, creating an environment that feels comfortable and accessible. The human scale is evident in the design of traditional Japanese tea houses, where the low ceilings and intimate spaces are intended to create a sense of coziness and tranquility. By aligning the scale of a building with the dimensions of the human body, architects can create spaces that feel inviting and relatable.

Proportion, on the other hand, refers to the relationship between different elements within a design. It is the art of balancing various components to create a cohesive whole. Proportion is a key factor in achieving visual harmony, as it ensures that no single element dominates the composition. The use of proportion can be seen in the design of classical architecture, where the careful arrangement of columns, pediments, and other elements creates a sense of order and symmetry.

The golden ratio is a mathematical concept that has been used by architects for centuries to achieve perfect proportion. This ratio, approximately 1.618, is often found in nature and is believed to be inherently pleasing to the human eye. Architects have used the golden ratio to guide the proportions of their designs, creating buildings that are both beautiful and harmonious. The Parthenon in Athens is a prime example of the golden ratio in architecture, with its façade and interior spaces carefully proportioned to reflect this mathematical principle.

In addition to the golden ratio, architects also use other systems of proportion to guide their designs. The modular system, developed by the architect Le Corbusier, is one such example. This system is based on the dimensions of the human body and uses a series of mathematical relationships to create a harmonious design. By using a consistent system of proportion, architects can ensure that their designs are cohesive and balanced.

The interplay between scale and proportion is essential in creating architectural harmony. When these principles are applied effectively, they can transform a building into a work of art, evoking a sense of beauty and balance. However, achieving this harmony requires a deep understanding of the relationship between different elements and a keen eye for detail.

One of the challenges architects face when working with scale and proportion is the need to balance functionality with aesthetics. While it is important to create a visually pleasing design, the building must also meet the practical needs of its occupants. This requires a careful consideration of how different elements interact and how they contribute to the overall function of the space.

For example, in the design of a public building, architects must consider the scale of the entrance and circulation spaces to ensure that they can accommodate large numbers of people. At the same time, these spaces must be proportioned in a way that creates a welcoming and inviting atmosphere. By carefully balancing scale and proportion, architects can create spaces that are both functional and beautiful.

Another consideration is the cultural context in which a building is situated. Different cultures have different perceptions of scale and proportion, and architects must be sensitive to these differences when designing buildings in diverse settings. For example, in some cultures, large and imposing structures may be seen as a symbol of power and authority, while in others, they may be perceived as oppressive or intimidating. By understanding the cultural context, architects can create designs that resonate with the local community and reflect their values and traditions.

The use of scale and proportion is not limited to the exterior of a building. These principles are also essential in the design of interior spaces. The arrangement of furniture, the height of ceilings, and the size of windows all contribute to the overall sense of harmony within a space. By carefully considering these elements, architects can create interiors that are both functional and aesthetically pleasing.

In recent years, advances in technology have provided architects with new tools for exploring scale and proportion. Computer-aided design software allows architects to experiment with different proportions and scales, enabling them to visualize and refine their designs before construction begins. This technology has opened up new possibilities for creating innovative and harmonious designs that push the boundaries of traditional architecture.

Despite these technological advancements, the fundamental principles of scale and proportion remain as relevant as ever. They provide a foundation upon which architects can build, allowing them to create spaces that are both functional and inspiring. By understanding and applying these principles, architects can design buildings that not only meet the practical needs of their occupants but also enrich their lives through beauty and harmony.

The Impact of Light and Shadow

Light and shadow are the silent architects of our world, shaping the way we perceive and interact with our surroundings. In the realm of architecture, these elements play a pivotal role in defining the character and mood of a space. They are the tools that architects wield to create depth, texture, and atmosphere, transforming static structures into dynamic environments that engage the senses and evoke emotion.

The interplay of light and shadow begins with the sun, the most powerful source of natural light. As it moves across the sky, the sun casts ever-changing patterns of light and shadow, altering the appearance of a building throughout the day. This dynamic quality is what makes natural light such a valuable asset in architectural design. By harnessing the sun's rays, architects can create spaces that are not only visually stunning but also energy-efficient and sustainable.

One of the most effective ways to utilize natural light is through the strategic placement of windows and openings. Large, south-facing windows can flood a space with sunlight, creating a warm and inviting atmosphere. Conversely, smaller, north-facing windows can provide a softer, more diffused light, ideal for creating a calm and contemplative environment. The size, shape, and orientation of windows can dramatically influence the quality of light within a space, allowing architects to tailor the lighting to suit the needs and functions of the building.

In addition to windows, architects can use other design elements to manipulate light and shadow. Overhangs, louvers, and screens can be employed to control the intensity and direction of sunlight, providing shade and reducing glare. These features not only enhance the comfort and usability of a space but also add visual interest and complexity to the building's façade. By carefully considering the interaction between light and shadow, architects can create a sense of rhythm and movement, drawing the eye and guiding the viewer's experience.

Artificial lighting is another crucial component of architectural design, offering a level of control and precision that natural light cannot. With the advent of LED technology, architects now have a vast array of lighting options at their disposal, from warm, ambient lighting to bright, focused task lighting. By layering different types of artificial light, architects can create a rich and nuanced lighting scheme that complements the natural light and enhances the overall atmosphere of the space.

The use of shadow is equally important in architectural design, providing contrast and definition to a space. Shadows can be used to highlight architectural features, such as columns, arches, and moldings, adding depth and dimension to the design. They can also be employed to create a sense of mystery and intrigue, drawing the viewer in and inviting them to explore the space further. By playing with light and shadow, architects can create a dynamic and engaging environment that captivates the imagination.

The impact of light and shadow extends beyond the visual realm, influencing the way we feel and behave within a space. Bright, well-lit spaces can evoke feelings of happiness and energy, while dimly lit environments can create a sense of intimacy and relaxation. The quality of light can also affect our perception of temperature, with warm, golden light creating a sense of warmth and comfort, and cool, blue light evoking a feeling of freshness and vitality. By understanding the psychological effects of light and shadow, architects can design spaces that not only look beautiful but also enhance the well-being and productivity of their occupants.

In addition to their aesthetic and psychological impact, light and shadow also play a practical role in architectural design. Properly designed lighting can improve visibility and safety, reducing the risk of accidents and injuries. It can also enhance the functionality of a space, providing the necessary illumination for tasks such as reading, cooking, and working. By considering the practical needs of the occupants, architects can create spaces that are both beautiful and functional.

The use of light and shadow is not limited to the interior of a building. Exterior lighting can be used to highlight the architectural features of a building, creating a striking visual impact and enhancing the building's presence within its surroundings. Landscape lighting can also be employed to illuminate pathways, gardens, and outdoor spaces, extending the usability of these areas into the evening hours. By thoughtfully integrating light and shadow into the exterior design, architects can create a seamless transition between the indoor and outdoor environments, enhancing the overall experience of the space.

The impact of light and shadow is a testament to the power of these elements to transform a space, creating an environment that is both visually stunning and emotionally resonant. By understanding and harnessing the interplay of light and shadow, architects can craft spaces that engage the senses, evoke emotion, and enhance the well-being of their occupants. Whether through the use of natural light, artificial lighting, or the strategic placement of shadows, the possibilities are endless, offering architects a rich palette with which to create their masterpieces.

Materiality Choosing the Right Elements

Materiality in architecture is akin to the palette of a painter, offering a spectrum of textures, colors, and properties that define the essence of a structure. The choice of materials is not merely a technical decision but a profound expression of the architect's vision, shaping the tactile and visual experience of a building. Selecting the right elements involves a delicate balance between aesthetics, functionality, sustainability, and cost, each factor playing a crucial role in the creation of a harmonious and enduring design.

The journey of material selection begins with understanding the context in which a building exists. The environment, climate, and cultural heritage of a location can significantly influence the choice of materials. In regions with harsh weather conditions, materials that offer durability and insulation, such as stone or brick, may be preferred. Conversely, in tropical climates, lightweight materials like bamboo or timber can provide natural ventilation and cooling. By considering the local context, architects can create designs that are not only visually appealing but also responsive to their surroundings.

Aesthetics play a pivotal role in material selection, as they contribute to the overall character and identity of a building. The texture, color, and finish of materials can evoke different emotions and perceptions, influencing how a space is experienced. Smooth, polished surfaces like glass or metal can convey a sense of modernity and sophistication, while rough, natural textures like wood or stone can create a warm and inviting atmosphere. The interplay of different materials can also add depth and complexity to a design, creating a rich tapestry of visual and tactile experiences.

Functionality is another critical consideration when choosing materials. Each material possesses unique properties that can enhance or hinder the performance of a building. For instance, concrete is renowned for its strength and versatility, making it ideal for structural elements. On the other hand, glass offers transparency and lightness, perfect for creating open and airy spaces. By understanding the strengths and limitations of each material, architects can make informed decisions that optimize the functionality and efficiency of their designs.

Sustainability has become an increasingly important factor in material selection, as architects strive to minimize the environmental impact of their projects. The use of sustainable materials, such as recycled steel, reclaimed wood, or low-VOC paints, can significantly reduce a building's carbon footprint. Additionally, locally sourced materials can decrease transportation emissions and support the local economy. By prioritizing sustainability, architects can create designs that not only respect the environment but also promote the well-being of future generations.

Cost is an inevitable consideration in the material selection process, as it directly impacts the feasibility and budget of a project. While high-end materials like marble or exotic hardwoods can add luxury and prestige to a design, they may not always be financially viable. Conversely, more affordable materials like concrete or plywood can offer cost-effective solutions without compromising on quality or aesthetics. By carefully balancing cost with other factors, architects can achieve a design that meets both the client's vision and budgetary constraints.

The integration of technology has opened new possibilities in material selection, allowing architects to experiment with innovative materials and techniques. Advanced composites, such as carbon fiber or engineered wood, offer enhanced performance and durability, while 3D printing technology enables the creation of complex and customized forms. These advancements provide architects with a broader palette of options, enabling them to push the boundaries of design and explore new creative possibilities.

The tactile experience of a building is deeply influenced by the choice of materials, as they engage the senses and create a connection between the occupant and the space. The cool touch of marble, the warmth of timber, or the roughness of exposed concrete can evoke different sensations and emotions, enhancing the overall experience of a building. By considering the sensory qualities of materials, architects can create spaces that resonate with the occupants on a deeper, more personal level.

The longevity and maintenance of materials are also important considerations, as they affect the durability and upkeep of a building over time. Materials that require minimal maintenance, such as stainless steel or ceramic tiles, can offer long-term cost savings and convenience. Conversely, materials that require regular upkeep, like natural wood or certain types of stone, may demand more attention and resources. By evaluating the maintenance requirements of materials, architects can ensure the longevity and sustainability of their designs.

The cultural and historical significance of materials can add a layer of meaning and context to a design, connecting it to its surroundings and heritage. Traditional materials like adobe, thatch, or terracotta can evoke a sense of place and continuity, while contemporary materials like glass or steel can symbolize progress and innovation. By thoughtfully incorporating culturally significant materials, architects can create designs that honor the past while embracing the future.

Chapter 3

Form and Function

The Relationship Between Form and Function

The relationship between form and function in design is a dynamic interplay that has long intrigued architects, designers, and artists alike. This intricate dance between aesthetics and utility is not merely a theoretical concept but a practical consideration that influences every aspect of the creative process. Understanding how form and function coexist and complement each other is essential for creating designs that are both visually appealing and purposefully effective.

At the heart of this relationship lies the principle that form should follow function, a concept popularized by the architect Louis Sullivan in the late 19th century. This idea suggests that the shape of a building or object should be primarily based upon its intended purpose. For instance, a chair is designed to support the human body comfortably, and its form reflects this function through its ergonomic shape and supportive structure. However, this principle is not a rigid rule but rather a guiding philosophy that encourages designers to prioritize functionality while still considering aesthetic appeal.

The balance between form and function can be observed in nature, where organisms have evolved to optimize their structures for survival. The streamlined shape of a fish, for example, reduces water resistance, allowing it to swim efficiently. Similarly, the intricate patterns of a butterfly's wings serve both as camouflage and as a means of attracting mates. These natural examples demonstrate how form and function are intertwined, each influencing and enhancing the other.

In architecture, the relationship between form and function is particularly evident. Buildings must not only be visually striking but also serve the needs of their occupants. A well-designed structure considers factors such as spatial layout, natural light, ventilation, and accessibility, all of which contribute to its functionality. The Guggenheim Museum in New York, designed by Frank Lloyd Wright, exemplifies this balance. Its iconic spiral form is not only visually captivating but also facilitates a unique viewing experience, guiding visitors through the exhibition space in a continuous flow.

The integration of form and function is also crucial in product design, where the usability and aesthetics of an object are paramount. Consider the design of a smartphone, which must be both visually appealing and easy to use. The sleek, minimalist form of modern smartphones reflects their advanced technological capabilities, while features such as touchscreens and intuitive interfaces enhance their functionality. By harmonizing form and function, designers create products that are both desirable and practical.

In the realm of fashion, the relationship between form and function is often more complex, as clothing serves both as a means of self-expression and as a practical necessity. Designers must consider factors such as comfort, durability, and versatility while also creating garments that reflect current trends and personal style. The little black dress, popularized by Coco Chanel, is a classic example of this balance. Its simple, elegant form allows for versatility and timeless appeal, while its functional design makes it suitable for a variety of occasions.

The tension between form and function can sometimes lead to creative breakthroughs, as designers seek innovative solutions to reconcile these two aspects. The development of sustainable materials and technologies has opened new possibilities for integrating form and function in environmentally conscious ways. For example, green roofs not only enhance the aesthetic appeal of a building but also provide insulation, reduce stormwater runoff, and promote biodiversity. By embracing sustainability, designers can create solutions that are both beautiful and beneficial to the environment.

The relationship between form and function is not static but evolves with cultural, technological, and societal changes. As new materials and technologies emerge, designers are challenged to rethink traditional notions of form and function, exploring new possibilities and pushing the boundaries of creativity. The rise of digital design tools and fabrication techniques, such as 3D printing, has expanded the designer's toolkit, enabling the creation of complex forms that were once unimaginable. These advancements allow for greater experimentation and customization, blurring the lines between form and function in exciting and innovative ways.

Ultimately, the relationship between form and function is a dialogue, a conversation between the designer and the user, the creator and the environment. It is a process of exploration and discovery, where each informs and enriches the other. By embracing this dynamic interplay, designers can create works that resonate on multiple levels, engaging the senses, fulfilling practical needs, and inspiring the imagination.

Functionalism in Modern Architecture

Functionalism in modern architecture emerged as a response to the rapid industrialization and urbanization of the late 19th and early 20th centuries. This architectural philosophy prioritizes the purpose and utility of a building over ornamental aesthetics, advocating for designs that are straightforward, efficient, and devoid of unnecessary embellishments. The movement gained momentum as architects sought to address the practical needs of a growing population while embracing new materials and construction techniques.

The roots of functionalism can be traced back to the influential work of architects such as Louis Sullivan, who famously coined the phrase "form follows function." This principle became a cornerstone of modern architecture, emphasizing that the design of a building should be dictated by its intended use. Sullivan's approach was revolutionary at the time, challenging the prevailing architectural norms that favored elaborate decoration and historical styles. His work laid the groundwork for a new generation of architects who would further develop and refine the concept of functionalism.

One of the most prominent figures in the functionalist movement was Le Corbusier, a Swiss-French architect whose innovative designs and theoretical writings had a profound impact on modern architecture. Le Corbusier advocated for a radical rethinking of urban living, proposing the use of standardized, prefabricated building components to create efficient, high-density housing. His vision was encapsulated in his concept of the "machine for living," which emphasized the importance of functionality and efficiency in residential design. Le Corbusier's iconic works, such as the Villa Savoye and the Unité d'Habitation, exemplify his commitment to functionalism, with their clean lines, open floor plans, and integration of modern materials like concrete and steel.

The Bauhaus school, founded by Walter Gropius in Germany, played a crucial role in the development and dissemination of functionalist principles. The Bauhaus emphasized the integration of art, craft, and technology, promoting a holistic approach to design that prioritized functionality and simplicity. The school's curriculum encouraged experimentation with new materials and construction techniques, fostering a spirit of innovation that would influence architects and designers worldwide. The Bauhaus aesthetic, characterized by its geometric forms, minimal ornamentation, and emphasis on practicality, became synonymous with modern architecture.

Functionalism also found expression in the work of Ludwig Mies van der Rohe, a German-American architect known for his minimalist approach and pioneering use of glass and steel. Mies van der Rohe's designs, such as the Barcelona Pavilion and the Seagram Building, exemplify the functionalist ethos with their emphasis on open spaces, structural clarity, and the honest expression of materials. His famous dictum "less is more" encapsulates the essence of functionalism, advocating for a reduction of form to its essential elements.

The impact of functionalism on modern architecture is evident in the widespread adoption of its principles in the design of public buildings, commercial spaces, and residential developments. Functionalist architecture is characterized by its emphasis on practicality, with features such as flat roofs, large windows, and open floor plans that maximize natural light and ventilation. The use of modern materials like reinforced concrete, steel, and glass allows for greater structural flexibility and the creation of innovative forms that challenge traditional architectural conventions.

Despite its many contributions to modern architecture, functionalism has faced criticism for its perceived lack of warmth and human scale. Critics argue that the emphasis on efficiency and standardization can result in sterile, impersonal environments that fail to address the emotional and social needs of their occupants. In response to these concerns, architects have sought to balance the functionalist ethos with a greater emphasis on human-centered design, incorporating elements such as natural materials, greenery, and communal spaces to create more inviting and livable environments.

The legacy of functionalism continues to influence contemporary architecture, as designers grapple with the challenges of sustainability, urbanization, and technological advancement. The principles of functionalism remain relevant in the quest for efficient, adaptable, and environmentally responsible design solutions. Architects are increasingly exploring the potential of new materials and construction methods, such as modular and prefabricated systems, to create buildings that are both functional and sustainable.

In the context of sustainable architecture, functionalism's emphasis on efficiency and resourcefulness aligns with the goals of minimizing environmental impact and optimizing energy use. The integration of passive design strategies, such as natural ventilation, daylighting, and thermal mass, reflects the functionalist commitment to creating buildings that respond to their environment and reduce reliance on mechanical systems. By prioritizing functionality and adaptability, architects can design spaces that are resilient to changing conditions and capable of meeting the diverse needs of their occupants.

The evolution of functionalism in modern architecture also reflects broader cultural and societal shifts, as architects seek to address issues of social equity, accessibility, and community engagement. The design of inclusive and adaptable spaces that accommodate diverse user needs is a testament to the enduring relevance of functionalist principles. By embracing a holistic approach to design that considers the social, cultural, and environmental context, architects can create spaces that are not only functional but also meaningful and enriching.

Case Studies Iconic Functional Designs

The world of architecture is replete with examples that embody the principles of functionalism, where form is dictated by purpose and utility. These iconic designs not only serve their intended functions but also stand as testaments to the innovative spirit of their creators. By examining these case studies, one can gain a deeper understanding of how functionalism has been applied in diverse contexts, resulting in structures that are both practical and aesthetically compelling.

One of the most celebrated examples of functionalist architecture is the Farnsworth House, designed by Ludwig Mies van der Rohe. Located in Plano, Illinois, this modernist masterpiece was commissioned by Dr. Edith Farnsworth as a weekend retreat. The house is a paradigm of simplicity and transparency, with its steel and glass construction allowing for an unobstructed connection with the surrounding landscape. The open floor plan and minimal interior partitions exemplify the functionalist ethos, creating a space that is both flexible and harmonious with nature. Mies van der Rohe's design emphasizes the honest expression of materials, with the structural elements left exposed to highlight their role in the building's form and function.

Another iconic functionalist design is the Villa Savoye, designed by Le Corbusier. Situated on the outskirts of Paris, this residential building is a quintessential example of Le Corbusier's "Five Points of Architecture," which include the use of pilotis (supporting columns), a flat roof terrace, an open floor plan, horizontal windows, and a free façade design. The Villa Savoye's design prioritizes functionality and efficiency, with its pilotis elevating the structure to create a seamless transition between the interior and exterior spaces. The open floor plan allows for flexible use of the interior, while the horizontal windows provide ample natural light and panoramic views of the surrounding landscape. Le Corbusier's design reflects his belief in the house as a "machine for living," where every element serves a specific purpose in enhancing the quality of life for its occupants.

The Bauhaus Dessau building, designed by Walter Gropius, is another landmark of functionalist architecture. As the home of the Bauhaus school from 1925 to 1932, the building embodies the principles of functionality, simplicity, and integration of art and technology. The design features a modular layout with distinct sections for workshops, classrooms, and living quarters, each tailored to their specific functions. The use of glass curtain walls allows for abundant natural light and visual transparency, fostering a sense of openness and collaboration. Gropius's design emphasizes the importance of adaptability and efficiency, with flexible spaces that can be reconfigured to accommodate changing needs.

In the realm of public architecture, the Sydney Opera House stands as a striking example of functionalism combined with expressive form. Designed by Danish architect Jørn Utzon, the building's iconic sail-like shells are not merely decorative but serve to enhance the acoustics and functionality of the performance spaces within. The design process involved extensive collaboration with engineers and acousticians to ensure that the structure met the complex requirements of a world-class performing arts venue. The result is a building that is both visually stunning and highly functional, with its innovative design contributing to its status as a UNESCO World Heritage Site.

The Pompidou Centre in Paris, designed by Renzo Piano and Richard Rogers, is another example of functionalism in public architecture. The building's radical design features an "inside-out" approach, with structural and mechanical elements such as pipes, ducts, and escalators exposed on the exterior. This approach not only maximizes the interior space for exhibitions and cultural activities but also creates a dynamic and interactive façade that engages with the urban environment. The Pompidou Centre's design challenges traditional notions of architectural form, demonstrating how functionalist principles can be applied in bold and unconventional ways.

In the context of educational architecture, the Salk Institute for Biological Studies in La Jolla, California, exemplifies the functionalist approach. Designed by Louis Kahn, the institute's layout is organized around a central courtyard, with laboratory spaces on either side. The design prioritizes functionality and collaboration, with flexible laboratory spaces that can be adapted to accommodate evolving research needs. The use of concrete and teak wood creates a sense of permanence and warmth, while the open courtyard provides a tranquil setting for reflection and interaction. Kahn's design reflects a deep understanding of the relationship between form and function, creating a space that supports scientific inquiry and innovation.

The TWA Flight Center at John F. Kennedy International Airport, designed by Eero Saarinen, is a notable example of functionalism in transportation architecture. The building's distinctive wing-shaped roof and sweeping curves are not only visually striking but also serve to guide passengers through the terminal with ease and efficiency. Saarinen's design emphasizes the importance of flow and movement, with open spaces and clear sightlines that facilitate the passenger experience. The TWA Flight Center's innovative design has made it an enduring symbol of mid-century modernism and a testament to the potential of functionalist architecture to create spaces that are both practical and inspiring.

Balancing Aesthetics and Utility

The delicate dance between aesthetics and utility in design is a challenge that has captivated architects, designers, and creators for centuries. Striking the right balance between these two elements is crucial for crafting spaces and objects that are not only visually appealing but also serve their intended purpose effectively. This chapter delves into the intricate relationship between aesthetics and utility, exploring how they can coexist harmoniously to create designs that resonate with both form and function.

Consider the iconic example of the Barcelona Chair, designed by Ludwig Mies van der Rohe and Lilly Reich for the German Pavilion at the 1929 International Exposition in Barcelona. This chair epitomizes the seamless integration of aesthetics and utility. Its sleek, minimalist design is a testament to the modernist movement, with clean lines and a focus on simplicity. Yet, the chair is not merely a visual delight; it is also a functional piece of furniture, designed with ergonomic considerations to provide comfort and support. The use of high-quality materials, such as leather and stainless steel, further enhances its durability and usability, ensuring that it remains a timeless piece in both form and function.

In the realm of architecture, the Guggenheim Museum in Bilbao, designed by Frank Gehry, serves as a striking example of balancing aesthetics and utility. The museum's undulating, titanium-clad exterior is a masterpiece of contemporary architecture, drawing visitors from around the world with its sculptural beauty. However, Gehry's design is not solely focused on aesthetics; it also considers the practical needs of a museum. The interior spaces are thoughtfully designed to accommodate a diverse range of exhibitions, with flexible galleries that can be adapted to suit different types of artwork. The building's layout facilitates the flow of visitors, ensuring a seamless and engaging experience as they move through the museum.

The Apple iPhone is another example of a product that successfully marries aesthetics with utility. From its inception, the iPhone has been celebrated for its sleek, elegant design, characterized by smooth curves and a minimalist interface. Yet, its appeal extends beyond its appearance; the iPhone is also a highly functional device, equipped with advanced technology and user-friendly features that cater to a wide range of needs. The intuitive design of the iOS operating system, combined with the device's powerful hardware, ensures that users can navigate and utilize the phone's capabilities with ease. This harmonious blend of form and function has contributed to the iPhone's enduring popularity and influence in the world of technology.

In urban design, the High Line in New York City exemplifies the successful integration of aesthetics and utility in a public space. Originally an elevated railway track, the High Line has been transformed into a linear park that weaves through the city, offering a unique perspective on the urban landscape. The design of the park incorporates elements of nature and art, with carefully curated plantings and installations that enhance its visual appeal. At the same time, the High Line serves a practical purpose, providing a green space for recreation and relaxation in a densely populated area. The park's design encourages community engagement and interaction, with seating areas, pathways, and performance spaces that cater to a variety of activities.

The concept of balancing aesthetics and utility is also evident in the world of fashion. Consider the classic trench coat, a garment that has remained a staple in wardrobes for decades. Its design is both stylish and practical, with features such as a waterproof fabric, adjustable belt, and deep pockets that cater to the needs of the wearer. The trench coat's timeless appeal lies in its ability to adapt to changing fashion trends while maintaining its functional attributes. This balance ensures that it remains a versatile and enduring piece in the world of fashion.

In the field of product design, the Dyson vacuum cleaner is a prime example of how aesthetics and utility can be harmoniously integrated. The sleek, futuristic design of the Dyson vacuum is visually striking, with its transparent dustbin and bold color accents. However, its appeal is not limited to its appearance; the vacuum is also engineered for optimal performance, with innovative technology that enhances its cleaning capabilities. Features such as cyclonic separation and a bagless design contribute to its efficiency and ease of use, ensuring that it meets the practical needs of consumers.

The balance between aesthetics and utility is not always easy to achieve, and it often requires a thoughtful and iterative design process. Designers must consider a multitude of factors, including the intended use of the product or space, the needs and preferences of the user, and the cultural and environmental context in which the design will exist. By prioritizing both form and function, designers can create solutions that are not only visually appealing but also practical and meaningful.

The Future of Functional Design

The future of functional design is a landscape rich with potential, where innovation and practicality converge to redefine how we interact with the world around us. As technology advances and societal needs evolve, designers are challenged to create solutions that not only meet the demands of today but also anticipate the needs of tomorrow. This chapter delves into the emerging trends and technologies shaping the future of functional design, offering insights into how these developments will influence the way we live, work, and play.

One of the most significant trends in functional design is the growing emphasis on sustainability. As awareness of environmental issues increases, designers are prioritizing eco-friendly materials and processes in their creations. This shift is evident in the rise of sustainable architecture, where buildings are designed to minimize energy consumption and reduce their carbon footprint. Innovations such as green roofs, solar panels, and rainwater harvesting systems are becoming integral components of modern architecture, demonstrating a commitment to environmental stewardship. In product design, the use of recycled materials and biodegradable components is gaining traction, as consumers seek products that align with their values and contribute to a more sustainable future.

Another key trend shaping the future of functional design is the integration of smart technology. The proliferation of the Internet of Things (IoT) has opened up new possibilities for creating interconnected environments that enhance convenience and efficiency. Smart homes, for example, are equipped with devices that can be controlled remotely, allowing users to adjust lighting, temperature, and security settings with ease. This level of automation extends to urban design as well, with smart cities leveraging data and technology to optimize traffic flow, reduce energy consumption, and improve public services. The seamless integration of technology into our daily lives is transforming the way we interact with our surroundings, making them more responsive and adaptable to our needs.

The rise of personalized design is another trend that is reshaping the functional design landscape. As consumers increasingly seek products and spaces that reflect their individual preferences and lifestyles, designers are embracing customization as a key element of their work. Advances in digital fabrication techniques, such as 3D printing, have made it possible to create bespoke products tailored to the specific needs of the user. This level of personalization extends to interior design as well, with modular furniture and adaptable layouts allowing individuals to configure their living spaces to suit their unique requirements. By prioritizing personalization, designers are creating solutions that resonate with users on a deeper level, enhancing their overall experience and satisfaction.

In the realm of transportation, functional design is playing a crucial role in shaping the future of mobility. As urban populations continue to grow, the need for efficient and sustainable transportation solutions becomes increasingly urgent. Electric vehicles (EVs) are at the forefront of this movement, offering a cleaner alternative to traditional gasoline-powered cars. The design of EVs is evolving to prioritize not only energy efficiency but also user experience, with features such as autonomous driving capabilities and advanced infotainment systems becoming standard. Public transportation systems are also undergoing a transformation, with innovations such as high-speed rail and autonomous buses promising to revolutionize the way we travel within and between cities.

The future of functional design is also being influenced by the growing importance of health and well-being. As people become more conscious of the impact of their environments on their physical and mental health, designers are incorporating elements that promote wellness into their creations. In architecture, this trend is evident in the design of spaces that maximize natural light, improve air quality, and encourage physical activity. Biophilic design, which seeks to connect people with nature, is gaining popularity as a way to enhance well-being and reduce stress. In product design, ergonomic considerations are becoming increasingly important, with designers creating products that support healthy posture and movement.

The intersection of design and social impact is another area where functional design is making strides. Designers are increasingly recognizing their role in addressing social challenges and creating solutions that promote equity and inclusivity. This is evident in the design of public spaces that are accessible to people of all abilities, as well as products that cater to diverse needs and preferences. By prioritizing social impact, designers are contributing to a more equitable and inclusive society, where everyone has the opportunity to thrive.

Chapter 4
Spatial Dynamics

Understanding Spatial Relationships

Understanding spatial relationships is a fundamental aspect of design that influences how we perceive and interact with our environment. Whether it's the layout of a room, the arrangement of elements on a page, or the organization of a city, spatial relationships play a crucial role in shaping our experiences. By grasping the principles of spatial relationships, designers can create harmonious and functional spaces that enhance usability and aesthetic appeal.

At the core of spatial relationships is the concept of proximity, which refers to the distance between elements in a design. Proximity can influence how we group and interpret information, as elements that are close together are often perceived as related. This principle is widely used in graphic design, where the arrangement of text and images can guide the viewer's eye and create a sense of hierarchy. In interior design, proximity can affect how we navigate a space, with closely placed furniture encouraging interaction and socialization.

Another important aspect of spatial relationships is alignment, which involves the positioning of elements along a common axis. Alignment creates a sense of order and cohesion, making a design feel more organized and intentional. In architecture, alignment can be used to create visual connections between different parts of a building, enhancing the flow and continuity of the space. In web design, alignment helps to create a clean and professional appearance, with elements such as text and images neatly lined up to create a cohesive layout.

Balance is another key principle of spatial relationships, referring to the distribution of visual weight within a design. Balance can be achieved through symmetry, where elements are mirrored on either side of a central axis, or through asymmetry, where different elements are arranged to create a sense of equilibrium. In landscape design, balance can be used to create a harmonious composition, with plants and structures arranged to create a pleasing visual effect. In product design, balance can affect the usability and stability of an object, with well-balanced designs feeling more comfortable and intuitive to use.

Scale and proportion are also critical components of spatial relationships, influencing how we perceive the size and importance of elements within a design. Scale refers to the size of an element in relation to its surroundings, while proportion refers to the relationship between different parts of a design. In architecture, scale and proportion can affect how a building fits into its environment, with well-proportioned designs feeling more harmonious and integrated. In fashion design, scale and proportion can influence how a garment fits and flatters the wearer, with carefully considered proportions creating a more aesthetically pleasing result.

The concept of hierarchy is closely related to spatial relationships, as it involves the arrangement of elements to indicate their relative importance. Hierarchy can be established through size, color, contrast, and placement, guiding the viewer's attention and creating a clear visual structure. In graphic design, hierarchy is used to prioritize information, with headlines and key messages given prominence to ensure they are noticed first. In urban planning, hierarchy can influence the organization of a city, with major roads and landmarks serving as focal points that guide navigation and movement.

Negative space, or the empty space around and between elements, is another important consideration in spatial relationships. Negative space can create a sense of openness and clarity, allowing the viewer to focus on the essential elements of a design. In art and photography, negative space can be used to create a sense of balance and contrast, highlighting the subject and enhancing its impact. In interior design, negative space can affect how a room feels, with well-considered use of empty space creating a sense of calm and spaciousness.

Understanding spatial relationships also involves considering the context in which a design exists. The surrounding environment, cultural influences, and user needs can all impact how spatial relationships are perceived and experienced. In architecture, context can influence the choice of materials, colors, and forms, with designs that respond to their surroundings feeling more authentic and connected. In product design, context can affect how a product is used and perceived, with designs that consider the user's environment and lifestyle feeling more relevant and functional.

The Psychology of Space

The psychology of space delves into the profound impact that our surroundings have on our emotions, behaviors, and overall well-being. This intricate relationship between humans and their environments is a fascinating area of study, revealing how the design and organization of space can influence our mental states and interactions. By understanding the psychological principles that govern our perception of space, we can create environments that promote comfort, productivity, and happiness.

One of the fundamental concepts in the psychology of space is the idea of personal space, which refers to the physical distance we maintain between ourselves and others. This invisible boundary varies depending on cultural norms, personal preferences, and situational contexts. In crowded urban settings, for instance, people may become accustomed to smaller personal spaces, while in rural areas, larger distances might be the norm. The violation of personal space can lead to discomfort and anxiety, highlighting the importance of designing spaces that respect these boundaries. In office environments, for example, providing employees with adequate personal space can enhance focus and reduce stress, leading to increased productivity.

The concept of territoriality is closely related to personal space and involves the sense of ownership and control over a specific area. This psychological need for territory can manifest in various ways, from the personalization of a workspace with family photos and personal items to the establishment of boundaries in shared living spaces. Territoriality can foster a sense of security and identity, making individuals feel more comfortable and at ease in their environments. In educational settings, allowing students to personalize their desks or lockers can create a sense of belonging and ownership, enhancing their engagement and motivation.

Another critical aspect of the psychology of space is the influence of environmental factors such as lighting, color, and acoustics on our mood and behavior. Natural light, for instance, has been shown to boost mood and improve concentration, making it a valuable element in the design of workspaces and educational facilities. The use of color can also have a significant impact on our emotions, with warm colors like red and orange evoking energy and excitement, while cool colors like blue and green promote calmness and relaxation. In healthcare settings, the strategic use of color and lighting can create a soothing atmosphere that aids in patient recovery and reduces stress.

Acoustics play a crucial role in shaping our experience of space, with noise levels affecting our ability to concentrate and communicate. In open-plan offices, excessive noise can lead to distractions and decreased productivity, highlighting the importance of sound management in these environments. The use of sound-absorbing materials, such as carpets and acoustic panels, can help mitigate noise and create a more conducive atmosphere for work and collaboration. In residential spaces, the careful consideration of acoustics can enhance the comfort and tranquility of a home, promoting relaxation and well-being.

The layout and organization of space can also influence our behavior and interactions. Open and flexible layouts can encourage collaboration and socialization, while more structured and compartmentalized spaces may promote focus and privacy. In retail environments, the arrangement of products and pathways can guide customer behavior, influencing their purchasing decisions and overall experience. The strategic placement of seating areas, displays, and signage can create a welcoming and intuitive shopping environment that enhances customer satisfaction and loyalty.

Biophilic design, which incorporates natural elements into built environments, is another important consideration in the psychology of space. This approach recognizes the innate human connection to nature and seeks to create spaces that foster this relationship. The inclusion of plants, natural materials, and views of nature can enhance well-being and reduce stress, making biophilic design a valuable strategy in a variety of settings. In urban environments, the integration of green spaces and natural elements can improve air quality, reduce noise, and create a sense of tranquility amidst the hustle and bustle of city life.

The psychology of space also encompasses the concept of wayfinding, which involves the ability to navigate and orient oneself within an environment. Effective wayfinding design can enhance the usability and accessibility of a space, reducing confusion and frustration. The use of clear signage, intuitive layouts, and visual cues can guide individuals through complex environments, such as airports, hospitals, and shopping centers. In educational settings, wayfinding strategies can support students in navigating campus facilities, promoting independence and confidence.

Cultural and social factors also play a significant role in shaping our perception of space. Different cultures may have varying preferences for spatial organization, personal space, and territoriality, influencing how environments are designed and experienced. Understanding these cultural nuances is essential for creating spaces that are inclusive and respectful of diverse needs and preferences. In multicultural settings, the consideration of cultural factors can enhance the sense of belonging and community, fostering positive interactions and relationships.

Designing for Movement and Flow

Designing for movement and flow is an essential aspect of creating spaces that are not only functional but also harmonious and inviting. The way people move through a space can significantly impact their experience, influencing everything from their mood to their productivity. By carefully considering the principles of movement and flow, designers can craft environments that facilitate ease of navigation, encourage interaction, and promote a sense of well-being.

One of the key elements in designing for movement is understanding the natural pathways that people are likely to take. These pathways, often referred to as desire lines, are the routes that individuals instinctively choose based on convenience and efficiency. Observing these patterns can provide valuable insights into how a space is used and inform the design process. For instance, in a public park, the creation of winding paths that follow the natural contours of the landscape can enhance the visitor experience, encouraging exploration and engagement with the environment.

In interior spaces, the arrangement of furniture and fixtures plays a crucial role in guiding movement and flow. Open layouts that allow for unobstructed pathways can create a sense of spaciousness and freedom, while strategically placed elements can direct traffic and define zones within a space. In a retail setting, for example, the placement of displays and aisles can influence customer behavior, encouraging them to explore different sections of the store and discover new products. The use of visual cues, such as color and lighting, can further enhance the flow, drawing attention to key areas and creating a cohesive and inviting atmosphere.

The concept of flow extends beyond physical movement to encompass the psychological experience of being in a space. A well-designed environment can facilitate a state of flow, where individuals become fully immersed and engaged in their activities. This state is characterized by a sense of focus, creativity, and satisfaction, making it a valuable consideration in the design of workspaces and educational facilities. By minimizing distractions and providing the necessary tools and resources, designers can create environments that support concentration and productivity, enabling individuals to perform at their best.

Incorporating elements of nature into a space can also enhance movement and flow, creating a sense of connection and tranquility. Biophilic design, which integrates natural materials, plants, and views of nature, can improve air quality, reduce stress, and promote well-being. In urban environments, the inclusion of green spaces and natural elements can provide a welcome respite from the hustle and bustle of city life, encouraging people to move and interact with their surroundings. The use of water features, such as fountains and ponds, can add a dynamic element to a space, creating a soothing and calming atmosphere that invites exploration and relaxation.

The design of entrances and exits is another important consideration in creating movement and flow. These transition points serve as gateways between different areas, setting the tone for the experience that follows. A welcoming entrance can create a positive first impression, inviting individuals to enter and explore a space. The use of clear signage and intuitive layouts can guide individuals through complex environments, reducing confusion and frustration. In public buildings, the design of entrances and exits can also play a role in ensuring safety and accessibility, providing clear and efficient routes for evacuation in case of emergencies.

The integration of technology can further enhance movement and flow, providing innovative solutions for navigation and interaction. Smart systems, such as automated lighting and climate control, can adapt to the needs of the occupants, creating a comfortable and responsive environment. In commercial spaces, the use of digital displays and interactive kiosks can provide information and guidance, enhancing the customer experience and facilitating engagement. The incorporation of technology can also support sustainability efforts, optimizing energy use and reducing the environmental impact of a space.

Cultural and social factors are also important considerations in designing for movement and flow. Different cultures may have varying preferences for spatial organization and movement patterns, influencing how environments are perceived and used. Understanding these cultural nuances can inform the design process, creating spaces that are inclusive and respectful of diverse needs and preferences. In multicultural settings, the consideration of cultural factors can enhance the sense of belonging and community, fostering positive interactions and relationships.

Creating Intimate vs. Expansive Spaces

The art of creating intimate versus expansive spaces lies in the delicate balance between scale, proportion, and the emotional responses they evoke. Each type of space serves a distinct purpose, influencing how individuals interact with their environment and with one another. Understanding the nuances of these spatial dynamics allows designers to craft environments that cater to specific needs, whether fostering connection and coziness or inspiring awe and openness.

Intimate spaces are characterized by their ability to evoke a sense of warmth, comfort, and privacy. These environments often feature smaller dimensions, lower ceilings, and a close arrangement of elements that encourage interaction and engagement. The use of soft textures, warm colors, and ambient lighting can enhance the feeling of intimacy, creating a cocoon-like atmosphere that invites relaxation and reflection. In residential settings, intimate spaces such as reading nooks, alcoves, and cozy corners provide a retreat from the hustle and bustle of daily life, offering a sanctuary for solitude or quiet conversation.

The design of intimate spaces often involves careful consideration of scale and proportion. Furniture and fixtures should be appropriately sized to maintain a sense of balance and harmony, avoiding overwhelming the space. The arrangement of elements can also play a crucial role in fostering intimacy, with seating configurations that encourage eye contact and conversation. The inclusion of personal touches, such as artwork, photographs, and cherished objects, can further enhance the sense of connection and belonging, making the space feel uniquely personal and inviting.

In contrast, expansive spaces are designed to inspire a sense of freedom, openness, and grandeur. These environments often feature larger dimensions, high ceilings, and an abundance of natural light, creating a feeling of spaciousness and airiness. Expansive spaces are well-suited for activities that require movement and flexibility, such as gatherings, performances, and exhibitions. In public buildings, expansive spaces such as atriums, galleries, and auditoriums serve as focal points for social interaction and cultural exchange, accommodating large groups and diverse activities.

The design of expansive spaces often emphasizes the use of materials and finishes that enhance the sense of scale and openness. Reflective surfaces, such as glass and polished metals, can amplify natural light and create a sense of continuity between indoor and outdoor environments. The use of neutral color palettes and minimalist design elements can further accentuate the feeling of expansiveness, allowing the architecture and the surrounding landscape to take center stage. In commercial settings, expansive spaces can convey a sense of prestige and sophistication, creating a memorable impression on visitors and clients.

While intimate and expansive spaces serve different purposes, they can coexist harmoniously within a single environment, offering a variety of experiences and opportunities for interaction. The transition between these spaces can be achieved through thoughtful design elements, such as changes in ceiling height, flooring materials, and lighting levels. These transitions can create a sense of progression and discovery, guiding individuals through a sequence of experiences that cater to their needs and preferences.

The integration of nature can also play a significant role in shaping intimate and expansive spaces. In intimate settings, the use of natural materials, such as wood and stone, can enhance the sense of warmth and connection to the environment. The inclusion of indoor plants and greenery can add a touch of vitality and freshness, creating a calming and restorative atmosphere. In expansive spaces, the incorporation of large windows and open vistas can blur the boundaries between indoor and outdoor environments, inviting the beauty of nature into the space and enhancing the sense of openness and freedom.

Cultural and social factors are important considerations in the design of intimate and expansive spaces. Different cultures may have varying preferences for spatial organization and the degree of intimacy or openness they desire. Understanding these cultural nuances can inform the design process, creating spaces that are inclusive and respectful of diverse needs and preferences. In multicultural settings, the consideration of cultural factors can enhance the sense of belonging and community, fostering positive interactions and relationships.

The use of technology can further enhance the experience of intimate and expansive spaces, providing innovative solutions for customization and interaction. Smart systems, such as adjustable lighting and climate control, can adapt to the needs of the occupants, creating a comfortable and responsive environment. In commercial spaces, the use of digital displays and interactive kiosks can provide information and guidance, enhancing the customer experience and facilitating engagement. The incorporation of technology can also support sustainability efforts, optimizing energy use and reducing the environmental impact of a space.

The Role of Technology in Spatial Design

Technology has become an integral part of spatial design, transforming the way we conceive, create, and interact with our environments. From the initial stages of conceptualization to the final touches of execution, technology offers a plethora of tools and innovations that enhance the design process and the spaces themselves. The role of technology in spatial design is multifaceted, encompassing everything from digital modeling and visualization to smart systems and sustainable solutions.

Digital modeling and visualization tools have revolutionized the way designers approach spatial design. Software programs such as AutoCAD, SketchUp, and Revit allow designers to create detailed and accurate representations of their ideas, enabling them to experiment with different layouts, materials, and lighting conditions. These tools provide a virtual canvas where designers can explore the possibilities of a space, making adjustments and refinements with ease. The ability to visualize a design in three dimensions allows for a more comprehensive understanding of the spatial dynamics, helping designers to anticipate potential challenges and opportunities.

Virtual reality (VR) and augmented reality (AR) technologies take digital visualization a step further, offering immersive experiences that allow designers and clients to explore a space before it is built. VR and AR enable users to walk through a virtual environment, experiencing the scale, proportions, and ambiance of a design in real-time. This immersive experience provides valuable insights into how a space will function and feel, allowing for informed decision-making and collaboration between designers and stakeholders. The use of VR and AR can also enhance client presentations, providing a compelling and interactive way to communicate design concepts and ideas.

The integration of smart systems and technologies into spatial design has led to the creation of environments that are responsive, adaptable, and efficient. Smart systems, such as automated lighting, climate control, and security, can be programmed to adjust to the needs and preferences of the occupants, creating a comfortable and personalized environment. These systems can also optimize energy use, reducing the environmental impact of a space and contributing to sustainability efforts. The use of sensors and data analytics can provide valuable insights into how a space is used, informing future design decisions and improvements.

Sustainability is a key consideration in modern spatial design, and technology plays a crucial role in achieving sustainable outcomes. The use of energy-efficient materials and systems, such as solar panels, green roofs, and rainwater harvesting, can reduce the environmental footprint of a space and promote resource conservation. Technology can also support sustainable design practices through the use of digital tools that assess the environmental impact of different design options, allowing designers to make informed choices that align with sustainability goals. The integration of sustainable technologies into spatial design not only benefits the environment but also enhances the well-being and comfort of the occupants.

The role of technology in spatial design extends beyond the physical environment to include the social and cultural dimensions of a space. Digital platforms and social media can facilitate collaboration and communication between designers, clients, and communities, fostering a sense of connection and engagement. Online tools and resources can provide access to a wealth of information and inspiration, supporting the creative process and expanding the possibilities of design. The use of technology can also enhance the accessibility and inclusivity of a space, providing solutions that accommodate diverse needs and preferences.

The rapid pace of technological advancement presents both opportunities and challenges for spatial design. Designers must stay informed about the latest developments and trends, continuously updating their skills and knowledge to remain competitive and relevant. The integration of technology into spatial design requires a thoughtful and strategic approach, balancing innovation with practicality and functionality. Designers must consider the long-term implications of technological choices, ensuring that they align with the goals and values of the project and the needs of the users.

Chapter 5
Cultural and Historical Influences

The Impact of History on Modern Design

History has always been a profound source of inspiration and influence in the realm of modern design. The echoes of past eras resonate through contemporary aesthetics, shaping the way we perceive and create our environments. This interplay between history and modern design is a dynamic dialogue, where the past informs the present, and the present reinterprets the past. Understanding this relationship is crucial for designers seeking to create spaces that are both innovative and rooted in a rich tapestry of cultural and historical context.

The influence of history on modern design can be seen in the revival and reinterpretation of classic styles and motifs. Designers often draw upon historical periods, such as the elegance of the Victorian era, the simplicity of the Arts and Crafts movement, or the boldness of Art Deco, to infuse their work with a sense of timelessness and continuity. These historical references provide a framework within which designers can experiment and innovate, blending traditional elements with contemporary sensibilities to create spaces that are both familiar and fresh.

One of the most significant ways history impacts modern design is through the preservation and adaptation of architectural heritage. Historic buildings and structures serve as tangible links to the past, offering insights into the cultural, social, and technological contexts of their time. The adaptive reuse of these structures allows designers to honor and preserve their historical significance while repurposing them for modern use. This approach not only conserves valuable architectural heritage but also breathes new life into spaces, creating a harmonious blend of old and new.

The principles of sustainability and environmental consciousness, which are central to modern design, also have historical roots. Many traditional building techniques and materials were inherently sustainable, utilizing local resources and responding to the natural environment. By revisiting these historical practices, designers can incorporate sustainable solutions that are both effective and respectful of cultural heritage. This fusion of past and present knowledge fosters a design ethos that values longevity, resourcefulness, and ecological balance.

Cultural history plays a pivotal role in shaping modern design, influencing everything from color palettes and patterns to spatial layouts and materials. Designers often draw inspiration from the rich tapestry of cultural traditions, incorporating elements that reflect the identity and heritage of a place or community. This cultural resonance adds depth and meaning to a design, creating spaces that are not only visually appealing but also emotionally and intellectually engaging. By acknowledging and celebrating cultural history, designers can create environments that foster a sense of belonging and connection.

The impact of history on modern design is also evident in the way designers respond to historical narratives and events. The stories and experiences of the past can serve as powerful catalysts for creativity, prompting designers to explore themes of memory, identity, and transformation. This narrative-driven approach to design encourages a deeper engagement with the spaces we inhabit, inviting us to reflect on our own place within the continuum of history. By weaving historical narratives into the fabric of modern design, designers can create spaces that resonate with meaning and purpose.

Technological advancements have enabled designers to explore historical influences in new and exciting ways. Digital tools and techniques allow for the precise replication and reinterpretation of historical elements, facilitating a seamless integration of past and present. This technological capability expands the possibilities for creative expression, enabling designers to push the boundaries of what is possible while remaining grounded in historical context. The result is a rich and diverse design landscape that celebrates the interplay of tradition and innovation.

The impact of history on modern design is not limited to aesthetics and form; it also extends to the underlying philosophies and values that guide the design process. Historical movements such as Modernism and Postmodernism have shaped contemporary design thinking, challenging designers to question conventions and explore new paradigms. These intellectual legacies continue to influence the way designers approach their work, encouraging a spirit of inquiry and experimentation that drives the evolution of design.

Cultural Symbols in Architecture

Architecture serves as a canvas upon which cultural symbols are etched, reflecting the values, beliefs, and identities of societies throughout history. These symbols, embedded in the very fabric of buildings and structures, offer a glimpse into the cultural narratives that shape our world. They are not mere decorative elements; they are powerful conveyors of meaning, capable of evoking emotions, sparking dialogue, and fostering a sense of belonging. Understanding the role of cultural symbols in architecture is essential for anyone seeking to appreciate the depth and complexity of the built environment.

Cultural symbols in architecture often manifest through the use of motifs, patterns, and iconography that hold specific significance within a given culture. These symbols can be religious, political, or social in nature, and they serve to communicate messages that transcend language and time. For instance, the lotus flower, a symbol of purity and enlightenment in many Eastern cultures, is frequently incorporated into the design of temples and sacred spaces. Similarly, the use of geometric patterns in Islamic architecture reflects the cultural emphasis on unity, order, and the infinite nature of the divine.

The incorporation of cultural symbols in architecture is not limited to traditional or historical structures; it is a practice that continues to evolve and adapt in response to contemporary cultural dynamics. Modern architects often draw upon cultural symbols to create spaces that resonate with the identities and aspirations of the communities they serve. This approach fosters a sense of continuity and connection, bridging the gap between past and present while celebrating the diversity of human experience.

One of the most compelling aspects of cultural symbols in architecture is their ability to convey complex narratives and evoke emotional responses. These symbols can serve as powerful reminders of a community's history, struggles, and triumphs, offering a sense of identity and pride. For example, the use of indigenous motifs in the design of public buildings can honor the heritage and contributions of native peoples, fostering a sense of inclusion and respect. Similarly, the incorporation of national symbols in government buildings can evoke feelings of patriotism and unity, reinforcing a shared sense of purpose and belonging.

The use of cultural symbols in architecture also plays a crucial role in shaping the perception and experience of space. These symbols can influence the way individuals interact with and interpret their surroundings, creating environments that are both meaningful and memorable. By embedding cultural symbols into the design of a space, architects can create a sense of place that resonates with the values and aspirations of its inhabitants. This approach not only enhances the aesthetic appeal of a building but also enriches the overall experience of those who engage with it.

Incorporating cultural symbols into architecture requires a deep understanding of the cultural context and a sensitivity to the nuances of meaning and interpretation. Architects must navigate the complexities of cultural representation, ensuring that symbols are used respectfully and authentically. This process often involves collaboration with cultural experts, community members, and stakeholders to ensure that the design accurately reflects the cultural narratives it seeks to convey. By engaging with these diverse perspectives, architects can create spaces that are both culturally resonant and universally accessible.

The interplay between cultural symbols and architecture is not static; it is a dynamic and evolving relationship that reflects the changing nature of culture itself. As societies evolve and adapt to new challenges and opportunities, so too do the symbols that define them. This evolution is evident in the way architects reinterpret traditional symbols to address contemporary issues, such as sustainability, social justice, and technological innovation. By reimagining cultural symbols in new and innovative ways, architects can create spaces that are both rooted in tradition and responsive to the needs of the present.

The role of cultural symbols in architecture extends beyond the physical boundaries of buildings and structures; it encompasses the broader cultural landscape in which they exist. These symbols contribute to the creation of cultural landmarks and heritage sites that serve as focal points for community identity and memory. They provide a sense of continuity and connection, linking individuals to their cultural roots and fostering a sense of belonging and pride. By preserving and celebrating these symbols, architects can contribute to the cultural vitality and resilience of communities.

Global Influences and Local Adaptations

Architecture is a living testament to the confluence of global influences and local adaptations, a dynamic interplay that shapes the built environment in profound ways. As societies become increasingly interconnected, the exchange of ideas, styles, and technologies transcends geographical boundaries, leaving an indelible mark on architectural practices worldwide. Yet, amidst this global exchange, the importance of local context and cultural specificity remains paramount, as architects strive to create spaces that resonate with the unique identities and needs of the communities they serve.

The phenomenon of global influences in architecture can be traced back to ancient times, when trade routes facilitated the exchange of goods, ideas, and artistic styles across continents. The Silk Road, for instance, served as a conduit for the dissemination of architectural motifs and construction techniques between Asia, the Middle East, and Europe. This cross-cultural exchange enriched the architectural vocabulary of each region, resulting in a tapestry of styles that bore the imprint of diverse influences. Today, globalization continues to drive the flow of architectural ideas, as architects draw inspiration from a myriad of sources, from cutting-edge technologies to traditional craftsmanship.

While global influences offer a wealth of opportunities for innovation and creativity, they also present challenges in terms of cultural authenticity and relevance. The risk of homogenization looms large, as the proliferation of international styles threatens to erode the distinctiveness of local architectural traditions. To counter this, architects must engage in a process of thoughtful adaptation, integrating global influences in a manner that respects and enhances the local context. This requires a deep understanding of the cultural, environmental, and social factors that shape a community's identity, as well as a commitment to preserving the integrity of local architectural heritage.

Local adaptations in architecture are not merely a response to global influences; they are a reflection of the unique conditions and aspirations of a particular place. These adaptations manifest in various ways, from the choice of materials and construction techniques to the design of spaces that accommodate local customs and lifestyles. For example, in regions with hot and arid climates, architects may incorporate traditional cooling strategies, such as courtyards and wind catchers, into modern designs to enhance thermal comfort and energy efficiency. Similarly, in areas prone to seismic activity, architects may draw upon indigenous building practices that prioritize structural resilience and safety.

The process of local adaptation is inherently collaborative, involving dialogue and engagement with a diverse array of stakeholders, including community members, cultural experts, and environmental specialists. By incorporating local knowledge and expertise into the design process, architects can create spaces that are not only aesthetically pleasing but also culturally resonant and environmentally sustainable. This approach fosters a sense of ownership and pride among community members, as they see their values and traditions reflected in the built environment.

One of the most compelling examples of global influences and local adaptations in architecture is the phenomenon of vernacular architecture, which embodies the principles of sustainability, functionality, and cultural relevance. Vernacular architecture is characterized by its use of locally sourced materials, traditional construction methods, and designs that respond to the specific climatic and cultural conditions of a region. While vernacular architecture is often associated with rural or indigenous communities, its principles are increasingly being embraced by contemporary architects seeking to create sustainable and contextually appropriate designs.

The integration of global influences and local adaptations is not limited to the physical aspects of architecture; it extends to the social and cultural dimensions of space. Architects must consider how their designs will impact the social dynamics and cultural practices of a community, ensuring that spaces are inclusive, accessible, and conducive to social interaction. This requires a sensitivity to the diverse needs and preferences of different user groups, as well as a commitment to fostering a sense of belonging and community cohesion.

In the context of urbanization and rapid development, the balance between global influences and local adaptations becomes even more critical. As cities expand and evolve, architects face the challenge of creating spaces that accommodate growth while preserving the cultural and historical fabric of urban environments. This necessitates a holistic approach to design, one that integrates considerations of heritage conservation, environmental sustainability, and social equity. By embracing this approach, architects can contribute to the creation of vibrant, resilient, and culturally rich urban landscapes.

The interplay between global influences and local adaptations in architecture is a testament to the richness and diversity of human creativity. It reflects the capacity of architects to transcend boundaries, drawing upon a global reservoir of ideas while remaining grounded in the specificities of place. This dynamic process enriches the built environment, creating spaces that are both innovative and deeply rooted in the cultural narratives of the communities they serve.

Case Studies Culturally Significant Structures

The world is adorned with culturally significant structures that stand as monuments to human ingenuity, creativity, and the rich tapestry of history. These structures, each with its own story, reflect the values, beliefs, and aspirations of the societies that built them. They serve as a bridge between the past and the present, offering insights into the cultural and historical contexts that shaped their creation. By examining these structures, we can gain a deeper understanding of the diverse ways in which architecture has been used to express cultural identity and heritage.

One of the most iconic examples of culturally significant architecture is the Parthenon in Athens, Greece. Constructed in the 5th century BCE, this ancient temple was dedicated to the goddess Athena, the patron deity of the city. The Parthenon is a masterpiece of classical Greek architecture, embodying the principles of symmetry, proportion, and harmony. Its design reflects the values of the Athenian society, which prized beauty, balance, and order. The Parthenon also served as a symbol of Athenian democracy and power, representing the city's cultural and political achievements. Despite the ravages of time and conflict, the Parthenon continues to inspire awe and admiration, standing as a testament to the enduring legacy of ancient Greek civilization.

Moving eastward, the Taj Mahal in Agra, India, is another culturally significant structure that captivates the imagination. Built in the 17th century by the Mughal emperor Shah Jahan as a mausoleum for his beloved wife Mumtaz Mahal, the Taj Mahal is a stunning example of Mughal architecture. Its design incorporates elements of Persian, Islamic, and Indian architectural styles, reflecting the cultural syncretism of the Mughal Empire. The Taj Mahal is renowned for its exquisite marble inlay work, intricate carvings, and symmetrical gardens, which create a sense of serenity and beauty. Beyond its architectural splendor, the Taj Mahal is a symbol of love and devotion, embodying the emperor's deep affection for his wife. It stands as a cultural icon, attracting millions of visitors from around the world who come to marvel at its beauty and learn about its history.

In the heart of the Middle East, the Alhambra in Granada, Spain, is a culturally significant structure that showcases the artistic and architectural achievements of the Nasrid dynasty. This medieval palace and fortress complex was built in the 13th and 14th centuries, during the height of Islamic rule in Spain. The Alhambra is renowned for its intricate stucco work, ornate tile mosaics, and lush gardens, which reflect the Islamic aesthetic of harmony and balance. The architecture of the Alhambra is a testament to the cultural exchange between the Islamic and Christian worlds, as it incorporates elements of both traditions. The Alhambra also holds historical significance as a symbol of the coexistence and conflict between different cultures and religions in medieval Spain. Today, it stands as a UNESCO World Heritage Site, preserving the rich cultural heritage of the region.

Crossing the Atlantic, the ancient city of Machu Picchu in Peru is a culturally significant structure that offers a glimpse into the architectural and engineering prowess of the Inca civilization. Built in the 15th century, this mountaintop citadel is a marvel of stone construction, with its precisely cut stones fitting together without the use of mortar. Machu Picchu's design reflects the Inca's deep connection to nature, as the structures are harmoniously integrated into the surrounding landscape. The site is believed to have served as a royal estate or religious retreat, and its layout is thought to have astronomical and ceremonial significance. Machu Picchu is a symbol of Inca ingenuity and resilience, representing the cultural achievements of a civilization that thrived in the challenging environment of the Andes. It continues to be a source of fascination and inspiration for archaeologists, historians, and travelers alike.

In the realm of modern architecture, the Sydney Opera House in Australia stands as a culturally significant structure that has become an iconic symbol of the city and the nation. Designed by Danish architect Jørn Utzon and completed in 1973, the Sydney Opera House is celebrated for its innovative design and engineering. Its distinctive sail-like shells are a feat of architectural creativity, pushing the boundaries of what was possible at the time. The Sydney Opera House is not only a center for the performing arts but also a symbol of Australia's cultural identity and aspirations. It represents the country's commitment to artistic excellence and innovation, attracting visitors from around the world who come to experience its performances and admire its design.

Preserving Heritage Through Design

Preserving heritage through design is a delicate dance between honoring the past and embracing the future.

It involves a thoughtful approach to architecture and urban planning, ensuring that the cultural and historical significance of a place is maintained while allowing for modern advancements. This process requires a deep understanding of the cultural context, as well as a commitment to sustainability and innovation. By examining the principles and practices of heritage preservation, we can uncover the ways in which design can serve as a powerful tool for safeguarding our shared history.

One of the fundamental aspects of preserving heritage through design is the concept of adaptive reuse. This approach involves repurposing existing structures for new functions, breathing new life into buildings that might otherwise be abandoned or demolished. Adaptive reuse not only conserves resources and reduces waste but also maintains the historical and cultural essence of a place. For instance, an old factory might be transformed into a vibrant community center, retaining its industrial charm while serving a new purpose. This practice allows communities to preserve their architectural heritage while meeting contemporary needs.

Incorporating traditional design elements into new constructions is another way to preserve cultural heritage. By drawing inspiration from historical architecture, designers can create buildings that resonate with the past while addressing present-day requirements. This approach often involves using local materials and techniques, which not only supports regional economies but also ensures that new structures harmonize with their surroundings. For example, a modern building in a historic district might feature traditional rooflines or decorative motifs, creating a visual connection to the area's architectural legacy.

Community involvement is crucial in the preservation of heritage through design. Engaging local residents in the planning and decision-making process ensures that the cultural values and priorities of the community are respected. This collaborative approach fosters a sense of ownership and pride, encouraging residents to actively participate in the preservation of their heritage. Public workshops, surveys, and open forums can provide valuable insights into the community's vision for its future, guiding designers in creating spaces that reflect the collective identity of the area.

Sustainability is an integral component of heritage preservation. By incorporating environmentally friendly practices into the design and construction process, we can ensure that our cultural heritage is preserved for future generations. This might involve using energy-efficient materials, implementing green building technologies, or designing spaces that promote biodiversity. Sustainable design not only reduces the environmental impact of construction but also enhances the longevity and resilience of heritage structures.

The integration of technology in heritage preservation offers exciting possibilities for design. Digital tools such as 3D modeling and virtual reality can be used to document and analyze historical sites, providing valuable data for restoration and conservation efforts. These technologies enable designers to create accurate replicas of original structures, ensuring that even the most intricate details are preserved. Additionally, technology can enhance the visitor experience, offering interactive exhibits and immersive tours that bring history to life.

Education plays a vital role in preserving heritage through design. By raising awareness of the importance of cultural heritage and the role of design in its preservation, we can inspire future generations to value and protect their history. Educational programs, workshops, and exhibitions can provide opportunities for individuals to learn about the principles of heritage preservation and the impact of design on cultural identity. By fostering a culture of appreciation and respect for heritage, we can ensure that our shared history is cherished and preserved.

The preservation of heritage through design is not without its challenges. Balancing the demands of modern development with the need to protect historical sites requires careful consideration and negotiation. Conflicting interests and limited resources can pose significant obstacles, necessitating creative solutions and compromise. However, by prioritizing collaboration, sustainability, and innovation, we can overcome these challenges and create spaces that honor our past while embracing the future.

Chapter 6

Sustainability and Innovation

Principles of Sustainable Architecture

Sustainable architecture is a transformative approach to building design that prioritizes environmental responsibility, resource efficiency, and the well-being of occupants. It seeks to minimize the negative impact of construction on the natural world while creating spaces that are healthy, comfortable, and adaptable. By adhering to key principles of sustainable architecture, architects and designers can contribute to a more sustainable future, addressing the pressing challenges of climate change, resource depletion, and urbanization.

One of the core principles of sustainable architecture is energy efficiency. Buildings are significant consumers of energy, and reducing their energy demand is crucial for minimizing their environmental footprint. This can be achieved through various strategies, such as optimizing building orientation and form to maximize natural light and ventilation, using high-performance insulation and glazing to reduce heat loss, and incorporating energy-efficient systems and appliances. Renewable energy sources, such as solar panels and wind turbines, can also be integrated into building designs to generate clean energy on-site, further reducing reliance on fossil fuels.

Water conservation is another essential aspect of sustainable architecture. With water scarcity becoming an increasingly pressing issue worldwide, it is vital to design buildings that use water efficiently and responsibly. This can involve implementing rainwater harvesting systems, using low-flow fixtures and fittings, and incorporating greywater recycling systems to reuse water for non-potable purposes. Landscaping can also play a role in water conservation, with drought-tolerant plants and efficient irrigation systems helping to reduce water consumption.

Material selection is a critical consideration in sustainable architecture. The choice of materials can have a significant impact on a building's environmental performance, from the energy required to produce and transport them to their potential for reuse or recycling at the end of their life. Sustainable materials are those that are sourced responsibly, have a low environmental impact, and contribute to the health and well-being of occupants. Examples include reclaimed or recycled materials, rapidly renewable resources such as bamboo, and non-toxic, low-emission products that improve indoor air quality.

The concept of life cycle assessment is integral to sustainable architecture. This involves evaluating the environmental impact of a building throughout its entire life cycle, from the extraction of raw materials to construction, operation, and eventual demolition or reuse. By considering the full life cycle of a building, architects can make informed decisions that minimize negative impacts and maximize positive outcomes. This holistic approach encourages the use of durable, adaptable materials and designs that can be easily maintained, repaired, or repurposed over time.

Sustainable architecture also emphasizes the importance of creating healthy indoor environments. The quality of indoor air, lighting, acoustics, and thermal comfort can significantly affect the well-being and productivity of occupants. To promote a healthy indoor environment, architects can incorporate natural ventilation and daylighting strategies, use non-toxic materials and finishes, and design spaces that support physical activity and mental well-being. Biophilic design, which seeks to connect occupants with nature through the use of natural elements and patterns, can also enhance the quality of indoor environments.

Community and context are vital considerations in sustainable architecture. Buildings do not exist in isolation; they are part of larger ecosystems and communities. Sustainable architecture seeks to create spaces that are responsive to their local context, respecting the cultural, social, and environmental characteristics of the area. This can involve engaging with local communities in the design process, using local materials and construction techniques, and designing buildings that contribute positively to the surrounding environment and community.

Adaptability and resilience are key principles of sustainable architecture. As the world faces increasing uncertainty and change, buildings must be designed to adapt to evolving needs and conditions. This can involve designing flexible spaces that can be easily reconfigured for different uses, incorporating passive design strategies that enhance resilience to climate change, and using durable materials and construction methods that withstand extreme weather events. By prioritizing adaptability and resilience, sustainable architecture can create buildings that are not only environmentally responsible but also capable of thriving in a changing world.

Innovation and technology play a crucial role in advancing sustainable architecture. Emerging technologies and innovative design approaches can offer new solutions to the challenges of sustainability, from smart building systems that optimize energy use to advanced materials that enhance performance and reduce environmental impact. By embracing innovation and staying informed about the latest developments in sustainable design, architects can push the boundaries of what is possible and create buildings that set new standards for sustainability.

Education and advocacy are essential components of sustainable architecture. By raising awareness of the importance of sustainability in the built environment and advocating for policies and practices that support sustainable design, architects can contribute to a broader cultural shift towards sustainability. This can involve engaging with clients, communities, and policymakers to promote sustainable design principles, participating in professional organizations and networks that support sustainability, and sharing knowledge and best practices with peers and the public.

Sustainable architecture is a dynamic and evolving field that requires a commitment to continuous learning and improvement. By staying informed about the latest research, technologies, and trends in sustainable design, architects can ensure that their work remains relevant and effective in addressing the challenges of sustainability. This commitment to lifelong learning can involve participating in professional development opportunities, attending conferences and workshops, and engaging with the broader community of sustainable design practitioners.

Innovative Materials and Technologies

The world of architecture is undergoing a profound transformation, driven by the emergence of innovative materials and technologies that are reshaping the way we design and construct buildings. These advancements are not only enhancing the aesthetic and functional aspects of architecture but are also paving the way for more sustainable and efficient building practices. As we delve into the realm of cutting-edge materials and technologies, it becomes evident that the future of architecture is being defined by creativity, adaptability, and a commitment to environmental stewardship.

One of the most exciting developments in the field of architecture is the advent of smart materials. These materials possess the ability to respond dynamically to changes in their environment, offering unprecedented levels of adaptability and functionality. For instance, thermochromic materials can alter their color in response to temperature fluctuations, providing a passive means of regulating indoor temperatures and reducing energy consumption. Similarly, photochromic materials adjust their transparency based on light exposure, optimizing natural lighting and minimizing the need for artificial illumination. By integrating smart materials into building designs, architects can create structures that are not only visually striking but also energy-efficient and responsive to their surroundings.

Another groundbreaking innovation is the use of advanced composites, which combine multiple materials to achieve superior performance characteristics. These composites are often lightweight yet incredibly strong, making them ideal for applications where traditional materials may fall short. Carbon fiber-reinforced polymers, for example, are being used to construct everything from bridges to skyscrapers, offering exceptional strength-to-weight ratios and resistance to environmental degradation. The versatility of advanced composites allows architects to push the boundaries of design, creating structures that are both aesthetically pleasing and structurally sound.

The rise of 3D printing technology is also revolutionizing the construction industry, enabling the creation of complex architectural forms with unprecedented precision and efficiency. By using 3D printers to fabricate building components, architects can reduce material waste, lower construction costs, and accelerate project timelines. This technology is particularly beneficial for producing intricate designs that would be difficult or impossible to achieve using traditional construction methods. Moreover, 3D printing allows for the use of sustainable materials, such as recycled plastics and bio-based composites, further enhancing the environmental credentials of modern architecture.

In addition to these material innovations, the integration of digital technologies is transforming the way architects approach design and construction. Building Information Modeling (BIM) is a prime example of how digital tools are streamlining the architectural process, allowing for more efficient collaboration and decision-making. BIM enables architects, engineers, and contractors to work from a shared digital model, ensuring that all stakeholders have access to the most up-to-date information and can coordinate their efforts seamlessly. This technology not only improves the accuracy and efficiency of the design process but also facilitates the integration of sustainable practices, such as energy modeling and lifecycle analysis.

The Internet of Things (IoT) is another digital innovation that is reshaping the architectural landscape. By embedding sensors and connectivity into building systems, architects can create smart buildings that monitor and optimize their performance in real-time. IoT-enabled buildings can adjust lighting, heating, and ventilation based on occupancy patterns, reducing energy consumption and enhancing occupant comfort. Additionally, these smart systems can provide valuable data on building performance, enabling architects to refine their designs and improve the sustainability of future projects.

Biomimicry, the practice of drawing inspiration from nature to solve design challenges, is also gaining traction in the field of architecture. By studying the structures and processes found in the natural world, architects can develop innovative solutions that are both efficient and sustainable. For example, the design of the Eastgate Centre in Harare, Zimbabwe, was inspired by the self-cooling mounds of African termites. By mimicking the natural ventilation system of these mounds, the building is able to maintain a comfortable indoor climate without the need for conventional air conditioning, resulting in significant energy savings.

The exploration of new materials and technologies is not limited to the structural and functional aspects of architecture; it also extends to the realm of aesthetics. Architects are increasingly experimenting with unconventional materials and techniques to create visually striking and thought-provoking designs. For instance, the use of translucent concrete, which incorporates optical fibers to transmit light, allows for the creation of walls that appear solid during the day but glow with an ethereal luminescence at night. This fusion of form and function exemplifies the potential of innovative materials to redefine the visual language of architecture.

As architects continue to explore the possibilities offered by new materials and technologies, it is essential to consider the broader implications of these innovations. While the potential benefits are immense, there are also challenges to be addressed, such as the environmental impact of material production and the ethical considerations surrounding the use of digital technologies. By approaching these challenges with a spirit of curiosity and responsibility, architects can harness the power of innovation to create buildings that are not only beautiful and functional but also sustainable and socially responsible.

Designing for Environmental Impact

Designing with an awareness of environmental impact is no longer a choice but a necessity. As the world grapples with the consequences of climate change, architects and designers are increasingly called upon to create spaces that not only serve human needs but also respect and preserve the natural environment. This chapter delves into the principles and practices that guide environmentally conscious design, offering insights into how we can create buildings that harmonize with their surroundings and contribute to a sustainable future.

The foundation of environmentally responsible design lies in understanding the lifecycle of a building, from conception to demolition. This holistic approach considers the environmental impact of every phase, including material selection, construction processes, energy consumption, and eventual deconstruction. By adopting a lifecycle perspective, designers can make informed decisions that minimize negative environmental effects and maximize resource efficiency.

Material selection is a critical aspect of designing for environmental impact. The choice of materials can significantly influence a building's carbon footprint, energy efficiency, and overall sustainability.

Sustainable materials, such as reclaimed wood, recycled metal, and low-impact concrete, offer viable alternatives to traditional building materials. These options not only reduce the demand for virgin resources but also often come with lower embodied energy, meaning less energy is required for their production and transportation.

In addition to selecting sustainable materials, designers must also consider the principles of passive design. This approach leverages the natural environment to regulate indoor conditions, reducing the need for artificial heating, cooling, and lighting. By strategically orienting buildings to take advantage of natural light and prevailing winds, architects can create spaces that are comfortable and energy-efficient. Features such as thermal mass, natural ventilation, and shading devices further enhance the performance of passive design, allowing buildings to maintain stable temperatures with minimal energy input.

Energy efficiency is another cornerstone of environmentally conscious design. Buildings are responsible for a significant portion of global energy consumption, making it imperative to incorporate energy-saving technologies and practices. High-performance insulation, energy-efficient windows, and advanced HVAC systems can dramatically reduce a building's energy use. Additionally, integrating renewable energy sources, such as solar panels or wind turbines, can further decrease reliance on fossil fuels and lower greenhouse gas emissions.

Water conservation is equally important in the quest for sustainable design. With water scarcity becoming an increasingly pressing issue, architects must prioritize strategies that reduce water consumption and promote efficient use. Low-flow fixtures, rainwater harvesting systems, and greywater recycling are just a few of the techniques that can be employed to minimize a building's water footprint. By designing landscapes that incorporate native, drought-tolerant plants, designers can also reduce the need for irrigation and support local ecosystems.

The concept of biophilic design emphasizes the importance of connecting people with nature, recognizing that our well-being is intrinsically linked to the natural world. By incorporating elements such as natural light, greenery, and water features into building designs, architects can create environments that promote health, productivity, and emotional well-being. Biophilic design not only enhances the quality of indoor spaces but also fosters a deeper appreciation for the environment, encouraging occupants to adopt more sustainable behaviors.

Adaptive reuse is another strategy that aligns with environmentally responsible design. By repurposing existing structures rather than demolishing them, architects can preserve the embodied energy of a building and reduce the environmental impact associated with new construction. Adaptive reuse projects often breathe new life into historic or underutilized buildings, transforming them into vibrant spaces that meet contemporary needs while honoring their past.

Community engagement is a vital component of designing for environmental impact. By involving local communities in the design process, architects can ensure that projects address the unique needs and values of the people they serve. This collaborative approach fosters a sense of ownership and responsibility, encouraging communities to actively participate in the stewardship of their environment. Moreover, community-driven design often results in more resilient and adaptable spaces, as local knowledge and expertise are integrated into the planning process.

The integration of green infrastructure is another powerful tool for mitigating environmental impact. Green roofs, permeable pavements, and urban forests are examples of green infrastructure that can enhance biodiversity, improve air quality, and manage stormwater runoff. These features not only contribute to the ecological health of urban areas but also provide valuable social and economic benefits, such as increased property values and improved public health.

As we navigate the complexities of designing for environmental impact, it is essential to remain open to innovation and experimentation. The field of sustainable design is constantly evolving, with new technologies and methodologies emerging at a rapid pace. By staying informed about the latest advancements and embracing a spirit of curiosity and creativity, architects can continue to push the boundaries of what is possible, creating spaces that are not only functional and beautiful but also sustainable and regenerative.

Case Studies Pioneers in Sustainable Design

The world of architecture and design has witnessed a remarkable transformation over the past few decades, driven by a growing awareness of environmental issues and the urgent need for sustainable solutions. This chapter delves into the stories of pioneering architects and designers who have blazed trails in sustainable design, offering valuable lessons and inspiration for those embarking on their own journeys toward creating environmentally responsible spaces.

One of the most celebrated figures in sustainable design is Renzo Piano, an Italian architect renowned for his innovative approach to integrating technology and nature. Piano's work on the California Academy of Sciences in San Francisco stands as a testament to his commitment to sustainability. The building, which houses an aquarium, planetarium, and natural history museum, is a marvel of green architecture. Its living roof, covered with native plants, not only provides insulation but also serves as a habitat for local wildlife. The building's design maximizes natural light and ventilation, reducing energy consumption and creating a harmonious connection with the surrounding Golden Gate Park.

Another trailblazer in sustainable design is Shigeru Ban, a Japanese architect known for his use of unconventional materials and humanitarian efforts. Ban's Paper Log Houses, developed in response to natural disasters, exemplify his innovative spirit. Constructed from recycled cardboard tubes, these temporary shelters are not only cost-effective and easy to assemble but also environmentally friendly. Ban's work challenges conventional notions of architecture, demonstrating that sustainable design can be both practical and compassionate.

In the realm of urban design, the city of Curitiba in Brazil has become a model for sustainable urban planning, thanks in large part to the visionary leadership of former mayor Jaime Lerner. Under Lerner's guidance, Curitiba implemented a series of groundbreaking initiatives that transformed the city into a beacon of sustainability. The city's integrated public transportation system, featuring dedicated bus lanes and efficient routes, has significantly reduced traffic congestion and pollution. Additionally, Curitiba's extensive network of parks and green spaces enhances biodiversity and provides residents with access to nature, promoting a healthier and more vibrant urban environment.

The Bullitt Center in Seattle, designed by the Miller Hull Partnership, is often hailed as the greenest commercial building in the world. This six-story office building is a shining example of the Living Building Challenge, a rigorous standard for sustainable construction. The Bullitt Center generates its own energy through solar panels, collects and treats rainwater for all its water needs, and features composting toilets to minimize waste. Its design prioritizes occupant health and well-being, with abundant natural light, fresh air, and non-toxic materials. The Bullitt Center demonstrates that it is possible to create a net-positive building that not only meets but exceeds the highest standards of sustainability.

In Denmark, the architectural firm Bjarke Ingels Group (BIG) has gained international acclaim for its innovative and sustainable designs. One of their most notable projects is the CopenHill waste-to-energy plant in Copenhagen, which doubles as a public recreation area. The plant's sloping roof serves as a year-round ski slope, while its façade features a climbing wall and hiking trails. CopenHill exemplifies BIG's philosophy of "hedonistic sustainability," where environmental responsibility is seamlessly integrated with enjoyment and quality of life. By transforming a utilitarian facility into a vibrant community space, BIG has redefined the possibilities of sustainable design.

The work of these pioneers underscores the importance of creativity, collaboration, and a willingness to challenge the status quo in the pursuit of sustainable design. Their projects demonstrate that sustainability is not a one-size-fits-all approach but rather a dynamic and evolving field that requires innovative thinking and adaptability. By learning from their successes and embracing their spirit of experimentation, designers can continue to push the boundaries of what is possible, creating spaces that are not only environmentally responsible but also enriching and inspiring.

As we reflect on the achievements of these trailblazers, it is essential to recognize that sustainable design is a collective endeavor. It requires the collaboration of architects, engineers, urban planners, policymakers, and communities to create lasting change. By fostering a culture of sustainability and encouraging interdisciplinary partnerships, we can build a future where the built environment supports the health and well-being of both people and the planet.

The Future of Green Architecture

Green architecture, once a niche concept, has evolved into a pivotal force shaping the future of the built environment. As the world grapples with the challenges of climate change, resource depletion, and urbanization, the demand for sustainable solutions has never been more urgent. The future of green architecture promises to be a dynamic and transformative journey, driven by innovation, technology, and a deep commitment to environmental stewardship.

One of the most exciting developments in green architecture is the integration of cutting-edge technology to enhance sustainability. Smart buildings, equipped with advanced sensors and automation systems, are revolutionizing the way we interact with our spaces. These intelligent structures optimize energy consumption by adjusting lighting, heating, and cooling based on occupancy and weather conditions. By harnessing the power of data, smart buildings not only reduce their environmental footprint but also improve the comfort and well-being of their occupants.

The rise of renewable energy sources is another key factor shaping the future of green architecture. Solar panels, wind turbines, and geothermal systems are becoming increasingly common features in sustainable buildings. These technologies enable structures to generate their own clean energy, reducing reliance on fossil fuels and lowering greenhouse gas emissions. As renewable energy becomes more accessible and affordable, architects and designers are finding innovative ways to incorporate these systems into their projects, creating buildings that are not only energy-efficient but also visually striking.

Biophilic design, which seeks to connect people with nature, is gaining traction as a fundamental principle of green architecture. This approach emphasizes the use of natural materials, abundant greenery, and elements that mimic natural forms and patterns. By fostering a sense of connection to the natural world, biophilic design enhances the physical and mental well-being of building occupants. As urban areas continue to expand, the integration of biophilic elements in architecture offers a vital means of bringing nature back into our daily lives.

The concept of circular economy is also influencing the future of green architecture. This approach prioritizes the use of sustainable materials, waste reduction, and the recycling and repurposing of resources. Architects are increasingly adopting circular design principles, creating buildings that can be easily disassembled and reused at the end of their life cycle. By minimizing waste and maximizing resource efficiency, circular architecture contributes to a more sustainable and resilient built environment.

Urban agriculture is emerging as a powerful tool for promoting sustainability in cities. Rooftop gardens, vertical farms, and community gardens are transforming urban landscapes, providing fresh produce and green spaces for residents. These initiatives not only reduce the carbon footprint associated with food transportation but also enhance food security and promote biodiversity. As cities continue to grow, integrating urban agriculture into architectural design will play a crucial role in creating sustainable and livable urban environments.

The future of green architecture is also being shaped by a growing emphasis on social sustainability. This approach recognizes that sustainable design must address not only environmental concerns but also social and economic factors. Architects are increasingly focusing on creating inclusive and equitable spaces that promote community engagement and well-being. By prioritizing accessibility, affordability, and cultural relevance, green architecture can contribute to more just and resilient communities.

As the field of green architecture continues to evolve, collaboration and interdisciplinary partnerships will be essential. Architects, engineers, urban planners, policymakers, and communities must work together to develop innovative solutions that address the complex challenges of sustainability. By fostering a culture of collaboration and knowledge-sharing, the architecture community can drive meaningful change and create a more sustainable future for all.

Education and advocacy will also play a critical role in advancing the future of green architecture. By raising awareness of the benefits of sustainable design and promoting best practices, architects can inspire the next generation of designers to prioritize environmental responsibility. Educational programs and initiatives that emphasize sustainability will equip aspiring architects with the skills and knowledge needed to create innovative and impactful solutions.

The future of green architecture is a journey of continuous learning and adaptation. As new technologies and materials emerge, architects must remain open to experimentation and embrace a spirit of innovation. By pushing the boundaries of what is possible, the architecture community can create spaces that are not only environmentally responsible but also enriching and inspiring.